Kali Orexi!
A Taste of Greece

Loucas Zouppas

PublishAmerica
Baltimore

© 2006 by Loucas Zouppas.
All rights reserved. No part of this book may be reproduced, stored in a retrieval system or transmitted in any form or by any means without the prior written permission of the publishers, except by a reviewer who may quote brief passages in a review to be printed in a newspaper, magazine or journal.

First printing

ISBN: 1-4137-9274-X
PUBLISHED BY PUBLISHAMERICA, LLLP
www.publishamerica.com
Baltimore

Printed in the United States of America

Good luck
[signature]

A good meal is like a beautiful woman:
you have to be honest, gentle, thoughtful and accurate.

Preface

I had a crazy idea a while back, to put together a few Greek recipes that are favorites of mine, just for something new and different....

I had a lot of fun doing it and also, somehow, came close mentally to a lot of people, or at least everyone who has tried them.

I felt good about this project of mine and I think it was worth it. I hope you do also. The recipes are easy and very tasty. They are not very expensive, but are very different. You should try them too, and when you do, I am sure that you will have good luck with them.

After all, your success will be also mine.

Cookingly yours,
Loucas Zouppas

Chicken Phyllo Pie
(Kotopita)

2	Boneless Chicken Breasts
8	Sheets Phyllo Pastry
1 lb.	Butter
1	Large Onion, minced
1/2 lb.	Mushrooms, diced
2 tbsp.	Parsley
1	Garlic Clove, minced
1 tbsp.	Flour
1/4 cup	Dry White Vermouth
1/2 tsp.	Pepper
1 tsp.	Salt
2 tbsp.	Olive Oil
2 cups	Bread Crumbs
1/2 lb.	Feta Cheese

Method:

In a heavy skillet, melt 3 tbsp. of the butter and sauté the onion until golden. Remove from pan and set aside. In same skillet, melt another 3 tbsp. butter and sauté the mushrooms until all the liquid is absorbed. Add the remaining onions, parsley, and garlic and sauté for 1 minute. Stir in the flour and blend well.

Add the vermouth and stir over moderate heat until thickened. Season with salt and pepper. Remove the mushroom mixture and set aside. In the same skillet sauté the chicken breasts, cut in half, in olive oil until golden brown. Remove from heat. Melt remaining butter in small saucepan and spread out phyllo sheet stack under wet towel to keep from drying out. Brush 1 sheet of phyllo at a time with butter, sprinkle with bread crumbs, place a second sheet of phyllo over the first, butter and sprinkle with crumbs. Place the chicken on the lower half of the phyllo. Place 1/4 of the cheese mixture on the top of the meat and fold the sides over, envelope-style. Repeat with remaining. Butter the chicken rolls and place seam end down on a baking sheet. Bake in preheated oven at 350 degrees for 35-40 minutes.

Serves 4
Time 1 1/2 hours

Greek-style BBQ Lamb Chops
(Arni Tis Sharas)

12	Lamb Rib Chops
1/4 cup	Olive Oil
1 tsp.	Oregano
1 tsp.	Salt
1 tsp.	Pepper
1	Lemon, juice only

Method:

Preheat BBQ grill on high. Pour the olive oil into a baking dish 10" x 10" and add the pork chops, coating well with oil on all sides. Set aside for 30 minutes. Sprinkle with the spices. Cook on BBQ grill when good and hot, cooking on both sides until crisp. Remove from grill and immediately lace with lemon juice. Serve with boiled or baked potatoes and tomato wedges.

Serves 6
Time 1 hour

Greek Lamb and Onions
(Stifatho)

1/4 lb.	Butter
2 tbsp.	Olive Oil
6	Garlic Cloves
1 1/2 lbs.	Lean Stewing Lamb, cubed
2 tbsp.	Tomato Paste
1 1/2 cups	Dry Red Wine
1 tbsp.	Red Wine Vinegar
1 1/2 lbs.	Small Onions
3	Bay Leaves
1/4 tsp.	Cumin
1/4 tsp.	Cinnamon
1/4 tsp.	Salt
1/4 tsp.	Pepper

Method:

Heat 3 tbsp. of the butter and all the olive oil over medium heat in a 3 quart casserole dish. Add 2 small chopped onions, garlic, meat cubes and brown. Add tomato paste and stir well to coat the meat. Add the wine and enough hot water to cover the meat. Mix in the vinegar, bay leaves, cumin, cinnamon, salt and pepper. Stir well, cover and reduce heat to simmer for 2 hours. Check periodically. Place the remaining onions in hot water for a while, then slip the skins off. Boil in salted water (1 tsp. salt to a quart of water) covered for 3 minutes. Drain and rinse with cool water. Place remaining butter into a frying pan over medium heat and brown onions. Set aside. Meat is done when it breaks away with a fork. Serve with the onions and cooked rice.

Serves 4-6
Time 3 hours

Lamb with Baked Orzo
(Arni Giouvetsi)

3 lbs.	Lamb Leg or Shoulder, cubed
3 tbsp.	Tomato Paste
6 cups	Boiling Water
1	Large Onion, minced
1 lb.	Orzo Pasta
1 cup	Parmesan Cheese, grated
2 tsp.	Salt
1/2 tsp.	Black Pepper
1 tsp.	Oregano
1	Lemon, juice only

Method:

Preheat oven to 400 degrees. Place cubes of lamb into a roasting pan and sprinkle with lemon juice, salt, pepper, and oregano. Toss and bake in preheated oven for 40 minutes. Add 1 cup of water to roasting pan, turn oven heat down to 325 degrees and roast for 1 more hour. Remove meat, cover and set aside to keep warm. Skim excess fat and scum from broth in pan. Dilute the tomato paste in remaining 5 cups of boiling water. Add salt and the minced onion. Sprinkle in the orzo and bake uncovered in a 350 degree oven for 30 minutes, stirring occasionally, until the orzo can be pierced with a fork. Place half of the meat in the pan by pushing down into the pasta. Place the rest of the meat evenly on top of the orzo and bake for 15 minutes or until a light crust develops. Serve immediately, sprinkled with cheese.

Serves 6-8
Time 2 1/2 hours

Leg of Lamb Elaine
(Arni Elenis)

1-4 lb.	Leg of Lamb
1/4 lb.	Butter
4	Lemons, juice only
1	Large Onion
1 cup	Long Grain Rice
1 cup	Mushrooms, finely chopped
1/2 cup	Celery, finely chopped
1/2 cup	Green Peppers, finely chopped
4	Garlic Cloves, minced
2	Eggs
1/4 cup	Cream
1/4 tsp.	Salt
1/4 tsp.	Pepper
1 tsp.	Parsley
2	Bay Leaves
1 cup	Bread Crumbs
1 lb	Small Round Potatoes

Method:

Preheat oven to 375 degrees. Run the blade of a sharp knife along the bone in the leg of lamb. Very carefully remove the bone and spread the meat flat, trying to keep it in one piece. Sprinkle with salt and pepper and set aside. Heat half of the butter in a large frying pan and sauté the onions, peppers, mushrooms, celery, garlic and the raw rice for about 10 minutes. Remove from heat and add a pinch of salt and pepper, along with the bay leaf. Beat the eggs with a fork or a wire whisk for about 5 minutes or until well blended. Add the cream and mix well. Replace the frying pan on low heat and mix in the bread crumbs thoroughly. Add the egg and cream mixture and beat until stiff. Set aside. Place the mixture onto the center of the meat, being sure to fold in the left and right sides of the meat to overlap. Skewer or tie off to keep the meat sealed. Place meat in center of roasting pan and add 1/2 cup of water to surround. Place in preheated oven. Melt the remaining butter and mix it together with the lemon juice. Coat the meat with this, as it cooks, every 20 minutes or so. Cook for 2 1/2 hours. One half hour before meat is done, place the potatoes in the roaster with meat and let cook until golden brown. Sprinkle with parsley and serve.

Serves 6-8
Time 2 1/2 hours

Greek Apple Pie
(Milopitta)

1/2 cup	Walnuts
1/4 cup	Bread Crumbs
7 1/2 cups	Chopped Cooking Apples
1/2 cup	Raisins
1/2 cup	Sugar
1 tsp.	Cinnamon
1/4 tsp.	Nutmeg
3/4 cup	Melted Butter
1/2 lb.	Phyllo Pastry
1 tbsp.	Water

Method:

Toast walnuts for 10 minutes at 350 degrees. Cool slightly, then chop finely. Toss together with bread crumbs. Combine apples, raisins, sugar, cinnamon and nutmeg in a large bowl. Mix so the apples are well coated. Brush bottom of 13"x9" pan with melted butter. Fold phyllo leaves to fit into the pan (leave enough set aside to layer to fill the baking dish). Brush with butter and sprinkle with a scant tbsp. of the walnut mixture. Repeat until half the phyllo is used. Spread in the apple mixture, top with the remaining phyllo, which is buttered and sprinkled in the same manner as the bottom was. With a sharp knife, cut top 3-4 layers of phyllo through, once lengthwise and 5 times across. Brush with butter and sprinkle with water. Place in preheated 400 degree oven and bake. Reduce the heat to 350 degrees and bake for 50 minutes to 1 hour, or until pastry is golden brown and apples are tender. Remove the pan to rest on a wire cooling rack. Cut completely through on the markings. Pour the prepared syrup, cooled, over it. Serve warm.

Honeyed Apple Syrup

Combine 1/2 cup apple juice, 1/2 cup sugar and 1/2 tsp. lemon rind in saucepan. Bring to a boil, then simmer for 5 minutes. Remove from heat. Stir in 2-3 tbsp. of honey and let cool.

Serves 8-10
Time 2 hours

Almond Apricot Phyllo Tart
(Filo Me Amygthala)

1 1/2 cups	Flour
1/2 tsp.	Baking powder
1 1/2 cups	Butter
1/4 cup	Cognac
8 sheets	Phyllo Pastry
1 tsp.	Grated Lemon Rind
3 1/2 cups	Toasted Almonds
4 cups	Sugar
1/2 cup	Bread Crumbs
7	Eggs
1/2 cup	Apricot Preserve
1 2/3 cups	Water
1	Cinnamon Stick
1 tsp.	Lemon Juice

Method:

Melt and cool the butter. In a bowl, combine the flour and the baking powder. Combine the butter, cognac, 1 egg yolk, 3 tbsp. sugar and lemon rind. Stir well. Combine the wet ingredients into the flour ingredients and stir to make a soft dough. Press into a 13"x9" baking pan and bake on lowest rack in oven at 350 degrees for 15 minutes. Brush the top with apricot preserve and let cool. In a large bowl combine the toasted almonds, 1 cup of sugar and the bread crumbs. Set aside. In a separate bowl, beat 6 egg yolks until they are light. Fold into the almond mixture. Beat together the 6 egg whites with a pinch of salt until stiff peaks are formed. Fold 1/4 of the whites into the almond mixture at a time until all is combined gently. Set aside while you melt 1 cup of butter and have the 8 sheets of phyllo spread out beneath a damp tea towel to keep them from, drying out. Spread the almond mixture over the pre-baked crust and level with a spatula. Taking 1 sheet of phyllo at a time, brush with butter, fold lengthwise and place on top of almond mixture. Continue in this manner until done. Brush the top of tart with butter. With a sharp knife, cut the phyllo topping into 2" diamonds. Bake at 350 degrees for 40 minutes. In a saucepan combine the remaining 2 1/2 cups sugar, water, cinnamon stick and lemon juice. Bring to a boil over moderately low heat, stirring constantly. Let simmer for 15 minutes. Strain syrup over the cooked tart and let stand 24 hours before serving.

Serves 20
Time 2 hours

Pita Bread
(Peta)

1 pkg	Dry Yeast
4 cups	Flour
1 1/2 cups	Water
2 tbsp.	Olive Oil
1 tsp.	Salt
1/4 tsp.	Sugar

Method:

In a mixing bowl, combine 1 1/2 cups of the flour with the yeast. In a separate bowl, combine the water, oil, salt, and sugar. Mix well. Combine this with the yeast and flour. Beat at low speed with an electric beater for 1/2 minute, then beat at high speed for 3 minutes. Knead the remaining flour in by hand. Place in a clean, lightly oiled bowl and set in a warm place to rise. Cover and let rise for 45 minutes. Punch dough down and divide into 12 pieces, rolling each one into a ball. Let stand for 10 minutes. Flatten the balls into 5" diameter circles. Place on a baking sheet and cover. Let stand for 30 minutes. Bake the pita at 400 degrees in preheated oven for 10 minutes until puffed and golden brown. Wrap in foil and cool.

Makes 1 dozen
Time 1 1/2 hours

Lamb Phyllo Pie
(Arni Filopita)

2 tbsp.	Olive Oil
2	Medium Onions, chopped
5 cups	Ground Lamb, minced
1/4 cup	Fresh Mint, chopped
1 tsp.	Cinnamon
1/4 tsp.	Nutmeg
1 tsp.	Salt
3/4 cup	Pine Nuts
24 sheets	Phyllo Pastry
1 cup	Butter, melted

Method:

Heat oil in a large frying pan and add the onions and cook until softened. Add the meat and brown. Drain off excess fat and add mint, cinnamon, nutmeg, salt and pine nuts. Stir well and set aside. Separate boxed phyllo pastry sheets. Melt the butter and brush each sheet with butter and keep covered and stacked under a wet tea towel to keep from drying until ready to use. Line a buttered baking dish 9"x13" with 4 sheets of phyllo that have been brushed with butter. Allow the ends of the phyllo to hang over the dish. Spread 1/4 of the lamb mixture over the phyllo and top with 4 more sheets in the same manner.

Continue to layer in this way until you end off with phyllo layers last. Brush top sheets with remaining butter and tuck the excess edges into sides of pan to enclose filling completely. Bake in a preheated oven at 375 degrees for 45 minutes or until golden brown. Serve hot with fresh bread and a good wine!

Serves 10
Time 1 1/2 hours

Lamb Stew with Broad Beans
(Arni Me Koukia)

2 lbs.	Lamb Stew Meat
4-19 oz.	Cans of Broad Beans
2	Medium Onions
4	Sprigs Parsley
2	Bay Leaves
2	Garlic Cloves
1 tsp.	Salt
1 tsp.	Celery Salt
1 tsp.	Pepper
1 cup	Olive Oil
1 qrt.	Water
2 tbsp.	Tomato Paste

Method:

Clean and cube the meat. Finely chop the onions, parsley and garlic. Preheat the olive oil in a heavy skillet and add chopped vegetables and spices, along with the bay leaves, celery salt, salt and pepper. Let simmer for about 10 minutes. Add the meat and brown for about 20 more minutes. Dilute the tomato paste into 1 quart water. Add to the meat in the saucepan and let simmer until meat is tender. Place the drained and rinsed beans into the pot and lower the heat. Let simmer for 20 minutes more. Remove from heat.

Serves 6
Time 3 hours

Lamb Fricassee

4 lbs.	Lamb Shoulder, cubed
6	Potatoes, peeled and cleaned
6	Small Onions, peeled
6	Medium Carrots
3	Celery Stalks, chopped
2	Eggs
1 cup	Angel Hair Pasta
1 tsp.	Salt
1/2 tsp.	Pepper
1	Lemon, juice only

Method:

Place cubed lamb in a large casserole dish and add enough water to cover. Add spices and let simmer for 45 minutes. Add vegetables and let simmer for another hour. Remove the meat and vegetables from the broth, and set aside. Add the pasta to the broth, being sure to stir occasionally. Let cook for 15 minutes. Beat together the eggs in a small bowl, adding the juice of 1 lemon slowly and gradually. Next add 1 cup of broth slowly, stirring constantly to mix. Add this mixture to the casserole with the remaining pasta and broth, stirring vigorously. Serve the pasta as a starter, then the meat and vegetables as a main dish.

Serves 6
Time 2 hours

Lamb with Wine Sauce
(Arni Krassato)

2 lbs.	Lamb Leg, cubed
1 tbsp.	Olive Oil
1 1/2 tbsp.	Flour
1	Garlic Clove, crushed
4	Lemon Wedges
1/4 cup	Dry White Wine
1/2 cup	Red Wine Vinegar
1 tbsp.	Butter
1 tsp.	Salt
1/2 tsp.	Pepper
1/2 tsp.	Rosemary
1/4 tsp.	Sage
1 tsp.	Minced Parsley

Method:

Heat the oil and butter in a heavy skillet. Add the lamb and sauté until browned. Lower the heat and add the remaining seasonings. Cook for 5 minutes. In a cup, mix the vinegar and white wine. Slowly stir in the flour. Add this flour mixture to the meat, stirring in well. Cover and cook over low heat for another 45 minutes until the lamb is tender. Serve with rice or pasta, decorated with lemon wedges and parsley.

Serves 4
Time 1 hour

Lamb with Lentils
(Arni Me Faki)

2 lbs.	Lamb Shoulder, cubed
1 1/2 cups	Onions, minced
1 cup	Tomatoes, peeled, seeded and chopped
1 cup	Lentils
2 1/2 cups	Beef Stock
4 cups	Salted Water
2 tbsp.	Butter
2 tbsp.	Olive Oil
2	Garlic Cloves, chopped
1	Bay Leaf
1 tsp.	Salt
1/2 tsp.	Pepper
1/2 tsp.	Rosemary, crushed
1 1/2 tbsp.	Flour

Method:

In a large skillet, heat the butter and olive oil. Add the lamb cubes and brown. Transfer the meat to a casserole dish, along with 1/3 of the oils. Sauté the onions and the garlic in the remaining oil in the skillet, until slightly browned. Sprinkle the flour into the onion mixture and continue to cook for another

3 minutes. Add the tomatoes, rosemary, bay leaf and salt and pepper, to taste. Stir until well mixed. Transfer the casserole dish to a preheated oven at 350 degrees and bake for 1 hour, covered. In a large saucepan, combine the lentils and the salted water. Simmer for 15 minutes, then drain. Remove the casserole dish from the oven, skim the fat from the broth and discard the bay leaf. Add the lentils in with the meat and continue to bake. Check periodically, adding more broth as required. Remove from oven when the lentils are tender. Sprinkle with parsley and serve.

Serves 8
Time 2 1/2 hours

Lamb Stuffed Cabbage
(Arni Gemisto Me Lahano)

3 lbs.	Savoy Cabbage
3 cups	Chicken Stock
1	Medium Onion, chopped
1	Carrot, chopped
1	Celery Stalk, chopped
8	Dill Stems
8	Parsley Stems
1	Bay Leaf
1/2 tsp.	Dried Thyme
1 1/2 cups	Tomato Sauce, canned

Stuffing:

3 cups	Ground Lamb Meat
1/2 cup	Cooked Rice
1/2 cup	Sultana Raisins
1/4 cup	Fresh Dill, snipped
1/4 cup	Toasted Pine Nuts
2	Large Eggs, beaten lightly
1 tbsp.	Garlic Cloves, minced
2 tsp.	Ground Cumin
1/2 tsp.	Cinnamon
1/8 tsp.	Ground Cloves
2 cups	Onions, minced
1/4 cup	Unsalted Butter

Method:

In a large bowl, combine the lamb, rice, raisins, dill, pine nuts, eggs, cumin, cinnamon, cloves, salt and pepper. In a skillet melt the butter over moderate heat. Add the onions and cook for about 3 minutes, until softened. Combine with remaining ingredients and mix well. Set aside. Blanche the cabbage for 10 minutes, drain and rinse with cold water. Place the cabbage stem side down on a double cheesecloth. Separate the leaves carefully, by pulling down. DO NOT REMOVE THE LEAVES FROM THE CABBAGE. When the leaves are pulled open and the core is exposed, cut out the core. Place half of the stuffing into center of the cabbage and, by using the cheesecloth, tie the cabbage together to maintain its shape. In a large casserole dish, combine 2 cups of the stock, onions, carrots, celery, dill stems, bay leaf and thyme. Place the wrapped cabbage into the pot, then pour remaining stock over top. Bring to a boil. Braise the cabbage, covered, with a buttered piece of foil and the lid, in a pre-heated oven at 375 degrees for 1 1/2 hours. Baste occasionally. Transfer to a colander and let stand for 10 minutes. Remove the cheesecloth and transfer to a heated platter. Drizzle with its own juices and serve.

Serves 8
Time 3 hours

Eggplant and Lamb Meatballs
(Melitzana Keftethes)

1 1/2 lbs.	Ground Lamb
1-8 oz.	Can Spiced Tomato Sauce
1/2 cup	Olive Oil
1/4 tsp.	Rosemary
1/2 tsp.	Dill
1 tsp.	Salt
1/2 tsp.	Pepper
1 tsp.	Parsley, minced
1	Egg
1/2 cup	Bread Crumbs
1	Garlic Clove, minced
1/2 cup	Onion, chopped
2 cups	Eggplant, peeled and chopped

Method:

Place all the ingredients together, with the exception of the oil and tomato sauce, into a large bowl. Shape the mixture into balls, any size. Heat a skillet with the oil and brown the meatballs on all sides. Drain off the excess fat and add the tomato sauce. Cover and simmer for 30 minutes. Serve hot.

Serves 6
Time 1 hour

BEEF STEW
(CREAS VOTHINO)

2 lbs.	Beef Chuck, Round or Blade Steaks, cubed
3 cups	Onions, sliced
2	Garlic Cloves, chopped
3 tbsp.	Olive Oil
6 oz. can	Tomato Paste
1-10 oz.	Can Beef Broth
1/4 cup	Red Wine Vinegar
1/2 tsp.	Salt
1/4 tsp.	Pepper
1 cup	Water
1/4 tsp.	Cinnamon
1	Bay Leaf

Method:

Preheat the oil over medium heat until it sizzles when water drops are sprinkled in. Place in the cubed meat, and brown well. Remove from pan and set aside. Brown onions and garlic in the same skillet. Return the meat back to the skillet now as well. Add the water, tomato paste, beef broth, vinegar, and seasonings. Mix well. Cover and simmer for 3-4 hours. Stir occasionally. Remove the bay leaf before serving.

Serves 6
Time 4 hours

Beef Stuffed Pita
(Vothino Kreas Me Pita Yemisto)

1 lb.	Sirloin Steak
2	Garlic Cloves, minced
1/2 cup	Dry Red Wine
1 cup	Plain Yogurt
2 tbsp.	Olive Oil
1/2 tsp.	Salt
1/4 tsp.	Pepper
2 tbsp.	Butter
4	Pita Bread Shells
3 cups	Lettuce, chopped
1 cup	Tomatoes, peeled and diced
1 cup	Cucumber, peeled and diced

Method:

Thicken the yogurt by placing it in a cheesecloth-lined strainer and letting it stand overnight in the refrigerator. Next day, combine the wine, oil, garlic, salt and pepper. Cut steak into 2" long strips and place into casserole dish. Pour over this the marinade and let stand for 1 hour. Drain the meat and cook in heavy frying pan until browned. Make a pocket in the pita by cutting open on one side. Serve meat in chafing dish to keep warm. Present the remaining ingredients in their own dishes as well. Allow your guests to make their own pitas.

Serves 4
Time 1 hour

Beef and Peas
(Bizelia Kima)

1 lb.	Ground Beef
1/2 cup	Parmesan Cheese
1 1/2 qrt.	Milk
6 tbsp.	Flour
1/3 lb.	Butter
1	Large Onion, chopped
1/4 tsp.	Nutmeg
1/4 tsp.	Ground Cloves
2 tbsp.	Parsley, minced
1-10 oz.	Can Peas
1 tsp.	Salt
1/2 tsp.	Pepper

Method:

Sauté the beef, onions, cloves, nutmeg, salt and pepper in butter until brown. Sprinkle with parsley and set aside. Cook peas by covering with water, bring to boil and drain. In a separate saucepan melt the butter. Add the flour gradually, stirring as you do. Add the milk gradually as well. Stir until creamy. Fold in the parmesan cheese. In a lightly greased 2 quart casserole, pour in 1/3 of the cream mixture, half the ground beef and half of the peas. Continue in this fashion until you end up with the last of the cream on top. Bake for about 45 minutes in a preheated 375 degree oven. Serve hot.

Serves 4
Time 1 hour

Liver in Wine Sauce
(Sikotakia Me Krasi)

1 lb.	Liver, thinly sliced
1/2 cup	Dry Red Wine
1/4 tsp.	Salt
1/4 tsp.	Pepper
1/4 cup	Flour
1/4 cup	Olive Oil
3	Medium Onions, sliced very thin
1 1/2 cups	Boiling Water

Sprinkle of Marjoram, Oregano, or Rosemary

Method:

Rinse liver well and pat dry. Marinate in wine for 1 hour. Remove the liver and set aside. Keep the wine. Season the liver with salt and pepper, then coat well with flour. Preheat oil in large skillet and sauté the liver quickly (about 10 minutes). Remove from pan. Place onions into pan, cover and cook for 5 minutes on low heat. Add the wine into this, along with the boiling water and the herbs. Let cook for a few minutes. Return liver to the pan, lower the heat and simmer for 15 minutes. Serve hot.

Serves 4
Time 1 1/2 hours

Veal and Pasta
(Moshari Macaroni)

3 lbs.	Veal, boneless, cut into 6 strips
3/4 cup	Butter
1/4 cup	Onions, minced
2 lbs.	Tomatoes, peeled, seeded and chopped
1 lb.	Macaroni
1 tsp.	Salt
1/2 tsp.	Pepper
1/2 cup	Parmesan Cheese, grated

Method:

Season the veal slices with salt and pepper. Set aside. Melt the butter in a skillet and brown the meat on both sides. Add the tomatoes and onions. Cover and let cook for 1 1/2 hours. Check regularly and add water if necessary. Cook the macaroni according to package instructions. Remove the meat from the skillet and measure the remaining sauce from the pan. Add enough water to make 6 cups. Pour this water mixture into a large casserole dish. Drain the macaroni and add to the casserole dish. Place meat on top and bake in a preheated oven at 350 degrees for 15 minutes. Sprinkle with cheese and serve hot.

Serves 6
Time 2 hours

Veal with Olives
(Moshari Me Elies)

2 1/2 lbs.	Veal, cubed
1 cup	Black Kalamata Olives, pitted
1/2 cup	Flour
1/4 cup	Olive Oil
2-19 oz.	Cans Tomatoes, crushed
1/2 cup	White Wine
1	Medium Onion, chopped
1 tsp.	Salt
1/2 tsp.	Pepper
1 tbsp.	Fresh Parsley, minced

Method:

Season the veal cubes with salt and pepper and coat in flour. Preheat the olive oil in a heavy skillet. Brown the meat on all sides. Add the onion, wine, tomatoes and parsley. Cook covered for 45 minutes. Check for tenderness. Add the olives and continue to cook until all liquid is absorbed. Serve over rice.

Serves 6
Time 1 1/2 hours

Stewed Veal Steaks
(Fileto Moshari Tiganito)

2 1/2 lbs.	Veal shoulder, trimmed and sliced
1 cup	Flour
1/4 cup	Olive Oil
1/4 cup	Red Wine Vinegar
1 1/2 cups	Water
3	Garlic Cloves, minced
1 tsp.	Salt
1/2 tsp.	Pepper
1/2 cup	Fresh Parsley, minced

Method:

Coat the meat slices with flour. Preheat the oil in a heavy skillet and brown the meat on all sides. Sprinkle with vinegar and water to barely cover. Add garlic, salt and pepper. Cover and simmer until meat is tender and sauce is reduced and thick. Sprinkle with parsley and serve with mashed potatoes.

Serves 6
Time 1 hour

STUFFED TOMATOES, PEPPERS
TOMATES GEMISTES

Baked Chicken Breasts
(Stithia Kotas' Psita)

4	Chicken Breasts, skinless and boneless
1 1/2 cups	Plain Yogurt
3 tbsp.	Lemon Juice
4	Garlic Cloves, chopped
1 tsp.	Celery Salt
1 tsp.	Salt
1 tsp.	Pepper
1/2 cup	Butter
1 cup	Fine Bread Crumbs

Method:

Combine all the spices, lemon juice and yogurt. Coat the chicken breasts in this mixture and set aside for 4-6 hours in the refrigerator. Take the coated chicken and roll it in the bread crumbs. Grease a shallow baking pan and layer the chicken on the bottom. In a separate saucepan, melt half the butter and pour over the meat. Bake the chicken for 1 hour in a preheated oven at 375 degrees. Baste with remaining butter halfway through the baking time. Serve hot.

Serves 8
Time 2 1/2 hours

Chicken Rolls
(Kota Me Fillo)

1	Large Chicken, cut into stewing pieces
5	Large Onions, chopped
2	Stalks Celery, whole
3	Large Carrots, chopped
1 tsp.	Peppercorns
1 tsp.	Salt
1/2 tsp.	Pepper
1 lb.	Phyllo Pastry
3	Eggs
1/2 tsp.	Nutmeg
2 tbsp.	Parsley, minced
1 1/2 cups	Chicken Stock
2 cups	Celery, minced
1 1/2 lbs.	Butter

Method:

Clean and piece the chicken. Place into a deep pot. Add enough water to cover. Add the 2 celery stalks, carrots, peppercorns, salt and pepper. Bring to a boil. Reduce heat and continue to simmer for 1 1/2 hours. Remove from heat and set aside to cool. Separate the meat from the bones and skin. Chop the meat into fine pieces with a sharp knife or cleaver. In a separate saucepan, melt 1/4 cup of the butter. Add the minced celery and cook for 5 minutes. Add the onion and cook for another 5 minutes. Add the meat and chicken stock and continue to cook until all the liquids are absorbed. Remove from heat and cool. Add parsley, nutmeg, salt and pepper. Beat the eggs until stiff and fold into the chicken mixture. Set aside. Melt the remaining butter, being sure not to let it burn, and brush 5 sheets of phyllo by placing them one on top of the other. Place 1/5 of the chicken mixture into the center of this and fold the ends of the first sheet of pastry inwards. Roll the pastry up like a jelly roll. Place in a baking dish. Repeat with remaining 4 sheets of pastry, being sure to brush each one with butter. Bake in preheated oven at 350 degrees for 45 minutes. Brush with butter once more, and serve hot.

Serves 9-10
Time 2 1/2 hours

Chicken Pie
(Kotopita)

1	Roasting Chicken
2	Large Onions, sliced
1/2 cup	Milk
1/2 lb.	Butter, melted
5	Eggs
1 tsp.	Salt
1/2 tsp.	Pepper
1/2 tsp.	Nutmeg
1 pckg.	Phyllo Pastry
1 cup	Parmesan Cheese

Method:

Clean the chicken well and place in a deep pot. Cover with water. Add the onions and cook for 2 hours, removing the froth as it forms. Remove the chicken from the liquid and let cool. De-bone and cut meat into strips. Pass the stock through a sieve. Place the strained stock, meat and milk back into the pot and cook for 5 minutes. Remove from heat. Add parmesan cheese and stir well. Beat together the eggs, nutmeg, salt, pepper and add to the meat mixture in the pan. Line a 9"x9" baking dish with a couple sheets of phyllo, brush with melted butter and layer with the meat mixture. Continue in this manner, leaving a 2" overhand of the pastry on all sides of the dish, until all meat mixture is used. Fold the overhanging phyllo edges toward the center of the dish. Cover the top with the remaining phyllo. Brush with butter and place in a preheated oven at 350 degrees for 1 hour. Let cool for 10 minutes before serving.

Serves 8
Time 3 1/2 hours

GREEK-STYLE CHICKEN WITH ORZO
(KOTA KRITHARI)

1	Frying Chicken, cut in serving pieces
2 cups	Water
2	Medium Onions, minced
1 cup	Orzo
1 tsp.	Salt
1/2 tsp.	Pepper
1/2 cup	Parmesan Cheese, grated
2 cups	Plain Yogurt
1/2 cup	Butter

Method:

Place the onions and butter in a skillet and sauté for 2 minutes. Add the cleaned chicken pieces and brown. Slowly add the water and bring to a boil. Mix in the orzo, salt, and pepper and lower the heat and simmer covered for 40 minutes, or until orzo is cooked. Garnish with grated parmesan and serve with plain yogurt.

Serves 4
Time 1 hour

SHISHKEBAB, LAMB
ARNI SOUVLAKI

Mediterranean Chicken and Okra
(Kotopoulo Me Bamies)

1 lb.	Okra, trimmed
1/2 cup	Wine Vinegar
3/4 cup	Butter
8 lbs.	Chicken Wings, Drumsticks, and Thighs
1	Large Onion, finely chopped
1 1/2 cups	Tomatoes, peeled and chopped
1 tbsp.	Tomato Paste
1/2 cup	Dry White Wine
1	Bay Leaf
2	Cinnamon Sticks
1/2 tsp.	Sugar
1 tsp.	Salt
1/4 tsp	Pepper

Method:

Place okra in a bowl and pour vinegar over to coat. Let soak 30 minutes. Drain and rinse the okra well. Pat dry. Melt 4 oz. butter in a deep frying pan, add chicken and brown. Remove and set aside. Reduce heat of frying pan and sauté the garlic and onion until golden brown. Add tomatoes, tomato paste, bay leaf, cinnamon, sugar, salt and pepper. Mix well, cover and simmer for 20 minutes. Add the chicken and simmer 15 minutes. In a saucepan melt the remaining butter and fry the okra until gold and tender, shaking it as it cooks (do not stir). Remove the okra and combine it with the chicken. Cover and cook for 20 minutes. Remove bay leaf and cinnamon sticks. Serve with mashed potatoes.

Serves 6
Time 2 hours

Greek Garden Chicken
(Kotopoulo a La Greque)

1	Whole Frying Chicken
1/2 lb.	Butter
1	Large Onion, finely chopped
1 lb.	Tomatoes, coarsely diced
1	Large Zucchini, sliced into strips
2	Celery Stalks, diced
4	Garlic Cloves, crushed
1 tsp.	Ground Oregano
1 tsp.	Salt
1/2 tsp.	Pepper
2 cups	Water
1 lb.	Small Potatoes
1 cup	Green Pepper, diced
1 tsp.	Parsley

Method:

Wash the chicken well and cut into frying pieces. Place into a large deep casserole pan. Season with salt and pepper. Lay slices of butter on top of chicken pieces. Add 1 cup of water to the casserole and place in a preheated oven at 350 degrees for 1 1/2 hours. When golden brown, remove from oven and let cool for 5 minutes. Drain away excess fat and set aside. Place enough of the drained oils in a frying pan and sauté the garlic, onions, celery, zucchini, potatoes, green peppers and parsley for about 10 minutes. Add the tomatoes last and combine gently. Pour this mixture over the meat in the casserole pan. Sprinkle with oregano and place back in the oven for 30 minutes, stirring occasionally. Remove from oven and serve with either rice or pasta.

Serves 6
Time 2 1/2 hours

Stuffed Chicken with Lamb
(Kota Paragemisti)

3/4 lb.	Ground Lamb Meat
1/2 cup	Olive Oil
1 3/4 cup	Cooked Rice
1/2 cup	Pine Nuts
1 tsp.	Pepper
1/2 tsp.	Cinnamon
1/4 tsp.	Nutmeg
1/2 tsp.	Thyme
1	Whole Chicken (4 lbs.)

Method:

Place ground lamb in with 3 tbsp. oil in a heated heavy skillet. Brown. Add the rice, pine nuts, salt, pepper, thyme, nutmeg and cinnamon. Stir and let simmer for 2 minutes. Remove from heat and stuff into the 4 lb. chicken. Seal the opening of the bird and tuck the wings in. Place in a roasting pan with enough water to prevent burning. Sprinkle with salt and pepper. Place in preheated oven at 375 degrees for about 2 hours. Baste with oil at first, later with its own juices. Serve hot.

Serves 4
Time 2 1/2 hours

Roast Goose
(Hina Psiti)

1	Goose (12 lb.)
3	Lemons
1 tsp.	Salt
1/2 tsp.	Pepper

Stuffing:

3 cups	Chestnuts, chopped
1 tsp.	Salt
1/2 tsp.	Pepper
1/2 cup	Pine Nuts
1/4 cup	Parsley, chopped
1 tsp.	Sugar
1/2 cup	Milk
2 tsp.	Cinnamon
1 1/2 cups	Apples, chopped
1/2 cup	Butter
2	Medium Onions

Method:

Clean goose well, then place in roasting pan and sprinkle with salt, pepper and lemon juice. Poke the goose with the point of a small knife all over.

Stuffing:

Sauté the onions in butter, add the apples and cook for 2 minutes. Add the milk, sugar, cinnamon, parsley, pine nuts, salt, pepper and simmer for a few more minutes. Add the chestnuts and mix well. Remove from heat and let cool before stuffing. Fill goose cavity loosely. Tie off opening of bird. Roast in a preheated oven at 375 degrees and allow 30 minutes cooking time per pound of meat. Serve hot.

Serves 8
Time 3 hours

Festive Greek Turkey
(Galopoula Yemisti)

1	Turkey(15lb.)
2	Large Onions, finely chopped
4	Celery Stalks, finely chopped
1 lb.	Chestnuts, peeled and boiled
1/4 1b.	Pine Nuts
1/4 lb.	Black Currants
1/4 cup	Raisins
4 cups	Long Grain Rice
1 tbsp.	Parsley
2 tsp.	Salt
1 tsp.	Pepper
12	Cloves, whole
1 cup	Olive Oil
2 cups	Water

*Also needed is a kit to tie off the opening of the bird (available at most supermarkets; contains a large darning needle and twine).

Method:

Clean the bird well, removing the innards and placing them in a small pot. Add 1 cup of water and cook them for 30 minutes.

Let cool, then chop very finely. Set aside. Heat the oil in a large frying pan and sauté the onions, celery, chopped innards, pine nuts, raisins, currants, chestnuts, cloves, salt and pepper until golden brown. Combine the water and the rice and sprinkle with parsley. Let simmer for 5 minutes and remove from heat (do not cook all the way as it will be too mushy once cooked in the bird). Stuff the turkey with this mixture and sew up tightly. Place into a preheated oven at 350 degrees and cook covered until tender. Baste occasionally. Once tender, uncover and let brown.

Serves 8
Time 5 hours

Rabbit with Garlic
(Kouneli Skortho)

1	Rabbit (2 1/2 lb.)
1/2 cup	Olive Oil
1/2 cup	Dry White Wine
1/2 cup	Wine Vinegar
1 tsp.	Salt
1/2 tsp.	Pepper

Garlic Sauce:
2 tbsp.	Butter
4	Garlic Cloves, chopped

Method:

Clean the rabbit well and cut into pieces. Place in a large bowl with the salt, pepper and vinegar. Add cold water to cover and let stand for 4 hours. Rinse and season the meat. Heat the oil in a heavy skillet. Add the meat and fry on all sides until golden brown. Add the wine. Cover and let simmer until the meat is tender. Prepare the garlic sauce by sauteing the 4 cloves of chopped garlic in 2 tbsp. butter. Cook until brown. Spread over the meat and serve hot.

Serves 4
Time 3 hours

Baked Lamb Islander
(Psito Nisiotiko)

2 lbs.	Lamb Shoulder Meat
1 lb.	Feta Cheese
2 lbs.	Roma Tomatoes, peeled and sliced
1 tsp.	Salt
1/2 tsp.	Pepper
2 tbsp.	Olive oil

Method:

Trim the excess fat from the lamb roast. Cut the meat into cubes. Coat the inside of a casserole pan with oil. Place the meat inside. Crumble the feta cheese over the meat. Cover with slices of the tomato and sprinkle with salt and pepper. Sprinkle lightly with more oil. Bake uncovered in a preheated 350 degree oven for 2 hours, basting with its own juices frequently.

Serves 6
Time 1 hour

Baked Lamb with Cabbage
(Arni Psito Me Lahano)

1 1/2 lbs.	Lamb Shoulder Meat, boneless
2 tbsp.	Olive Oil
1 1/4 cups	Beef Stock
1 lb.	White Cabbage
2	Large Onions, diced
2 tsp.	Fresh Black Pepper
1 tsp.	Salt

Method:

Cut the lamb into 1 1/2 inch cubes. In a heavy skillet brown in 2 tbsp. heated oil. Remove from heat and place the meat into a bowl. Sprinkle with salt and pepper. In the same skillet, sauté 1 cup diced onion until softened. Place in a small dish and set aside. Drain the fat from the skillet and add 1 1/4 cups beef stock. Stir in the lamb meat and bring to a boil. Remove from heat. Rinse and chop up cabbage into 1" slices. Line the bottom of a 2 quart casserole pan with half the meat sprinkled with some of the onion, salt and pepper, then a layer of cabbage also sprinkled with salt and pepper. Continue in the same manner until all layers are complete. Pour the beef stock over this. Add a cheese cloth spice bag containing 2 tsp. peppercorns, crushed, and 1 bay leaf. Bake covered in a preheated oven at 350 degrees for 1 1/2 hours or until lamb is tender. Remove and discard the spice bag before serving.

Serves 4
Time 2 hours

Lamb with Artichokes
(Arni Me Aginares)

3 lbs.	Lamb Meat, any cut
2	Large Onions, chopped
4	Celery Stalks, diced
1/2 lb.	Small Carrots, sliced
1 bunch	Fresh Dill
1 lb	Small Potatoes, chopped into large pieces
1 tsp.	Salt
2 1/2 cups	Water
1/4 cup	Olive Oil
1/4 tsp.	Black Pepper
3-14 oz.	Cans Artichoke Hearts
1	Lemon, juice only

Method:

Sauté the onions, celery, salt, pepper and dill together for about 5 minutes. Add diced meat and brown. Add 2 cups hot water and lemon juice to this. Let simmer for 1 hour over low heat. Add veggies to the lamb. Bring to a boil for 25 minutes. When the veggies are tender, remove from the heat and serve.

Serves 6
Time 2 1/2 hours

Filet of Lamb
(Fileto Arni)

4	Pieces Lamb Filet, cut into 1" thickness
1 lb.	Squid Tubes, sliced lengthwise
1/2 cup	Butter
1/2 cup	Small Mushroom Caps
1 cup	Onion, chopped
4	Garlic Cloves, chopped
1 tsp.	Salt
1/2 tsp.	Pepper
1 tsp.	Parsley
1/2 tsp.	Oregano
1	Lemon, juice only

Method:

Wash the squid tubes well. Heat 1/4 cup of the butter in a skillet. Add the squid, mushroom caps, onions, garlic, parsley, oregano, salt and pepper and sauté for 10 minutes. Set aside. In another skillet melt the remaining butter on medium-high heat. Place the lamb filet into this and brown. Reheat the squid mixture for about 4 minutes. Squeeze in lemon juice just before removing from the heat. Cover. Place the lamb pieces on a serving platter and cover with a generous serving of the squid mixture. Serve with potatoes or rice.

Serves 4
Time 1 hour

Cheese Triangles
(Tyropitakia)

1 lb.	Feta Cheese
12 oz.	Dry Cottage Cheese
1/2 cup	Fresh Parsley, finely chopped
1/4 tsp.	White Pepper
1 tsp.	Dill
6	Eggs, room temperature, well beaten
1/2 lb.	Unsalted Butter
1 lb	Phyllo Pastry, room temperature

Method:

Rinse feta cheese under cold water, drain and crumble into a bowl. Blend in cottage cheese, parsley, dill and pepper. Add beaten eggs and mix well. Stir in onions and spinach. Gently unfold phyllo pastry. Using sharp clean scissors gently cut the phyllo stack into 3 equal lengthwise strips. Wrap 2 of the 3 stacks in plastic and refrigerate until needed. Cover remaining stack with damp towel, and work with one sheet at a time. Take first strip and gently fold both long sides in toward the middle of the strip. Brush with melted butter to keep from drying out. Place 1 tsp. of cheese mixture into the bottom left corner of the pastry strip. Fold this corner over so the bottom edge touches the right or left edge of the strip, forming a right-angle triangle. Continue in this manner until entire strip is folded to form a multi-layered triangle. Continue with remaining strips until everything is complete. Place on baking sheet, being sure not to let triangles touch. Brush again with melted butter and bake in preheated oven at 425 degrees until crisp and golden brown (about 12-15 minutes).

Serves 12-15
Time 3.5 hours

Yogurt Fruit
(Frouta Yaourti)

1 cup	Melon, cubed (Cantaloupe, Honey Dew or Watermelon)
1 cup	Orange Segments
1 cup	Peaches, sliced
1 cup	Whole Strawberries
1 cup	Grapes, seedless
1/4 cup	Slivered Almonds
1 cup	Plain Yogurt
3 tbsp.	Honey
1 1/2 tbsp.	Grated Lemon Rind

Method:

In a medium bowl, combine the yogurt, honey and lemon rind. In a separate bowl toss all the fruit together. Pour the yogurt mixture overtop and gently fold together. Serve ice cold.

Serves 6
Time 20 minutes

Watermelon Preserve
(Karpouzi)

3 lbs.	Watermelon Rind
4 1/2 cups	Sugar
1 1/2 cups	Honey
1 1/2 cups	Water
1 1/2 cups	Toasted Almond Slivers
6	Cinnamon Sticks
1 1/2	Lemons, juice only

Method:

Peel the outside off the rind, cube and place in a saucepan. Add the honey, water and cinnamon sticks. Simmer over low heat for 1 hour. Skim the top frequently of any foam that may form while cooking. Should reach the jelly stage. Add the almonds and the lemon juice when done. Pour into preserve jars that have been sterilized. Seal properly and let cool.

Time 1 hour

Greek Walnut Cake
(Karithopita)

1/2 lb.	Unsalted Butter
2 cups	Sugar
2 tsp.	Vanilla
8	Eggs, room temperature
1 tsp.	Baking Powder
1/2 tsp.	Baking Soda
2 tsp.	Ground Cinnamon
1 cup	Farina or Cream of Wheat (not instant)
1 cup	Flour
1/2 cup	Milk
2 cups	Walnuts, coarsely chopped
3 cups	Water
1 cup	Honey
1	Orange, sliced with the peel on
1 tsp.	Lemon Juice
1/2	Cinnamon Stick

Method:

Butter a 13"x9" brownie pan. Preheat the oven to 375 degrees. Cream the butter and half the sugar until fluffy. Add vanilla and eggs. Beat for 2 minutes. Add the baking soda, baking powder and cinnamon and beat for another 2 minutes. Combine the flour, cream of wheat, milk and walnuts in a separate bowl. Mix well. Combine the butter mixture with the flour mixture stirring gently. Pour the batter into the greased pan, and smooth with a spatula. Bake for 40 minutes.

Syrup

Prepare while cake is in the oven. Combine the remaining cup of sugar and ingredients into a saucepan. Bring to boil, stirring constantly. Reduce the heat and simmer until cake is done (toothpick should come out clean from center). Remove cinnamon stick and orange slices. Slowly pour syrup over the cake, 1 cup at a time, allowing the first to soak in before adding the next cup. Allow to sit for at least 4 hours before serving. Cut into squares and serve with expresso or tea.

Serves 10
Time 1 hour

Turkish Delight
(Loukoumi)

2 tbsp.	Gelatin
1 cup	Water
1	Lemon
1	Orange
3 cups	Sugar
2/3 cup	Cornstarch
1 kg. box	Icing Sugar
	Green or Red Food Coloring

Method:

Sprinkle gelatin over 4 tbsp. water and set aside to soften. Peel lemon and orange, being sure not to leave any white pith. Squeeze and strain the juice from the fruit into heavy saucepan. Place the rinds in as well, along with the granulated sugar and 2/3 cup water. Stir to dissolve sugar before bringing to a rolling boil. Boil steady without stirring for a full 4-5 minutes until mixture is thick. To test it, drop 1/2 tsp. of the syrup into a cup of cold water. If it forms long threads it is ready. Mix cornstarch with remaining cold water and add to syrup with the softened gelatin. Simmer until clear and gelatin has dissolved, stirring occasionally. Add a few drops of food coloring and strain into a lightly oiled 7" shallow tin pan. Leave to set overnight. Cut into squares the next day and roll in sifted icing sugar. Package in layers and separate with wax paper lightly dusted with icing sugar.

If you wish, you may add nuts to this recipe. Simply chop up either walnuts, pistachios, or almonds and add to the mixture before pouring to set overnight.

Greek Short Bread Cookies
(Kourabiethes)

1 lb	Unsalted Butter
1	Egg Yolk
1/4 cup	Icing Sugar, sifted
1/3 cup	Blanched Almonds, finely chopped
1/2 tsp.	Almond Extract
1 tsp.	Baking Powder
1 tbsp.	Brandy
6 cups	Flour
	Whole Cloves
	Icing Sugar

Method:

Cream the butter until fluffy. Add egg yolk, 1/4 cup icing sugar, nuts and flavoring. Mix well. Add the flour and baking powder and mix well by kneading together for 5 minutes. Using walnut-sized pieces of dough, shape into crescents. Place on ungreased cookie sheet. Insert 1 whole clove into each cookie. Bake at 350 degrees for 12-15 minutes, until bottom edges are golden brown. Remove from cookie sheet to a well-dusted tray of icing sugar. Place in a single layer in the sugar. Cover with a generous dusting of icing sugar. Continue layering the baked cookies in this manner. Finish with another dusting of icing sugar and serve.

Makes 5 dozen
Time 1 1/2 hours

Saragli

1 1/2 lbs.	Walnuts
1/2 cup	Sugar
1 lb.	Unsalted Butter
3 tsp.	Cinnamon
1 tsp.	Cloves
2 lbs,	Phyllo Pastry
	Syrup

Method:

Place nuts, cinnamon, cloves and sugar in a bowl and mix well. Take 1 sheet of the phyllo pastry (keep the rest under a damp towel to keep moist). Brush the sheet with melted butter and cut in half from top to bottom. Spoon some of the mixture into the middle of half and spread out toward each side. Fold the sides in to keep mixture from spilling out. Fold the bottom edge up over some of the mixture. Place a dowel (handle of a wooden spoon works great) about 12" long across the pastry horizontally. Roll the pastry up over the dowel tightly like a jelly roll. Push both ends of the pastry toward the center, then slide the dowel out of the center just as you are placing the pastry into an ungreased brownie pan. This is called shirring. Shirr each pastry in the same manner, being sure to pack them tightly together in the pan. Brush with butter and bake in a preheated 350 degree oven for 40 minutes. Cut into 2" long pieces and dip each piece into the cold syrup. Let sit on wire cake rack.

Syrup

In a saucepan combine 4 cups sugar, 1 cup honey, 1 cinnamon stick, 1/2 cup lemon juice and 2 cups water. Simmer for about 30 minutes and skim off any foam that forms. Let cool and place in refrigerator to stiffen up for about 20 minutes before using.

Makes 48 pieces
Time 1 hour

Sesame Cookies
(Koulou Rakia)

1/2 lb.	Unsalted Butter
1 1/2 cups	Sugar
6	Eggs, one egg white aside
6 tsp.	Baking Powder
6 cups	Flour
1/2 tsp.	Salt
	Sesame Seeds
1 tsp.	Vanilla (or 2 tsp. Grated Orange Peel or 1 tsp. Nutmeg)

Method:

Cream butter and sugar until fluffy. Beat in eggs 1 at a time. Add your choice of flavoring. In a separate bowl, sift together baking powder, salt and flour. Add a little at a time to the butter mixture, making a stiff dough. Pinch a walnut-sized piece off and roll between your hands to shape into a twist. Place on a cookie sheet, brush with the slightly beaten egg white and sprinkle with sesame seeds. Bake at 350 degrees for 20-30 minutes or until golden brown.

Makes 2 dozen
Time 20 minutes

SHISKEBAB, SQUID
KALAMARI SOUVLA

Pecan Bars
(Karithia Tetragona)

4 cups	Pecans, chopped
4 cups	Flour
1 cup	Icing Sugar
2 tbsp.	Vanilla
2 tbsp.	Ice Water
2 cups	Butter

Method:

Cream the butter thoroughly. Add 8 tbsp. of the icing sugar and blend well. Mix the nuts and flour and add to the mixture. Add vanilla and ice water and blend well. Pinch off walnut-sized ball of dough and roll between hands to form 1" roll. Place on cookie sheet and bake in preheated oven at 325 degrees for 35 minutes. Sift remaining icing sugar over the cookies and place in a container to mellow.

Makes 4 dozen
Time 1 hour

Olive Muffins
(Eliopsoma)

1 1/4 lb.	Black Kalamata Olives, pitted and chopped
4 cups	Flour
2 tbsp.	Sugar
2 tbsp.	Baking Powder
2 tsp.	Dried Crushed Mint
2 cups	Olive Oil
2	Onions, grated

Method:

Combine all ingredients, with the baking powder last. Brush muffin tins with oil and dust with flour. (Do not use paper baking cups.) Fill the cups 3/4 full with batter and bake for 45 minutes at 350 degrees. Serve warm.

Makes 3 dozen
Time 1 hour

Greek New Year's Cake
(Hristopsomo a La Greque)

3 cups	Flour
6	Eggs
2 tsp.	Baking Powder
2 cups	Sugar
1/2 lb.	Butter
1/2 tsp.	Baking Soda
1/4 cup	Lemon Juice
1/2 cup	Chopped Walnuts
1 cup	Milk
1/2 cup	Berry Sugar

Method:

Cream butter and sugar until light. Add the flour and mix well. Add the eggs 1 at a time, beating well. Combine together the milk and the baking powder. Add this to the egg mixture. Combine together the soda and lemon juice and mix into the main mixture. Place batter into a 10"x9" greased layer cake pan. Preheat the oven to 350 degrees and bake for 20 minutes. Sprinkle with nuts and berry sugar and continue baking for 30 minutes longer.

Serves 8-10
Time 1 hour

Kadaife
(Kadaifi)

1 cup	Walnuts, chopped
1 cup	Almonds, chopped
1/4 cup	Sugar
1/4 cup	Rusk Crumbs
1/8 tsp.	Ground Cloves
1 oz.	Cognac
1 lb.	Kadaife
3/4 cup	Sweet Butter, melted
1 tsp.	Cinnamon

Syrup:

4 cups	Sugar
2 1/2 cups	Water
1	Cinnamon Stick
1/2	Lemon, juice and rind

Method:

Combine all syrup ingredients in heavy saucepan and bring to a boil. Lower heat and let simmer for 20 minutes. Set aside to cool. Combine the nuts, crumbs, sugar, cinnamon, cloves and cognac in a bowl. Separate the strands of kadaife and form 24 rectangular sections 12" long and 3" wide. Place 1 tbsp. of the nut mixture on 1 end of each strand and roll tight like a jelly roll. Place in a casserole dish and continue in same manner until all mixture is used. Pour 1 tsp. of melted butter over each roll and bake in preheated oven at 350 degrees until golden brown. Pour the cool syrup over the baked rolls and let stand for a while before serving.

Serves 12
Time 1 1/2 hours

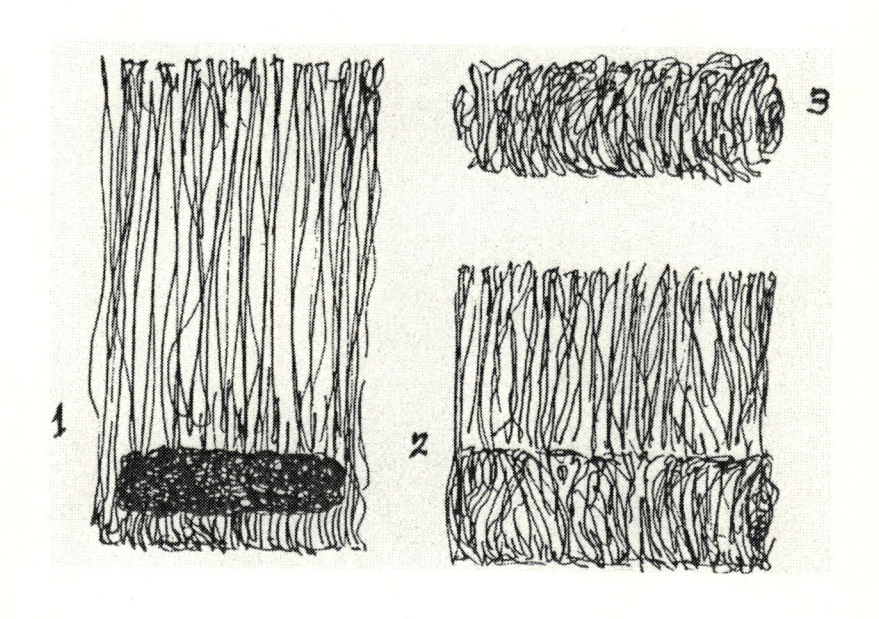

NOODLES

Greek-Style Fish Balls
(Keftethakia Psari)

2 cups	Cod, cooked
2	Eggs
1 cup	Bread Crumbs
1/2 cup	Parmesan Cheese
1	Onion, minced
1 cup	Water
1 tbsp.	Fresh Mint, minced
1 tsp.	Salt
1/2 tsp.	Pepper
1 cup	Flour
1 cup	Olive Oil
2	Lemon, juice only

Method:

Preheat the olive oil in a heavy skillet. Crumble the cooked fish into a bowl together with the mint leaves, onion, bread crumbs, cheese, water, eggs, salt and pepper. Mix well. Form balls, roll them in flour and cook in the preheated oil until golden brown. Serve hot with tartar sauce, Russian dressing, or lemon juice.

Serves 6
Time 30 minutes

GREEK-STYLE LAMB CHOPS
(PAITHIA ARNI)

4	Garlic Cloves, mashed
2	Zucchini, medium sized and chopped
1	Green Pepper, chopped
1	Medium Onion, chopped
1/2	Lemon
1 tsp.	Salt
1 tsp.	Pepper
1	Large Tomato, chopped
12	Lamb Chops

Method:

Dice the garlic, zucchini, onions, green pepper and lemon. Set aside. Cut a deep pocket in through the side of each lamb chop. Stuff the pocket full of the mixture of vegetables. These can be cooked on the BBQ or in a roasting pan in the oven at 375 degrees. Cook until golden brown, basting frequently with lemon juice from remaining half of lemon. Serve with fresh parsley, french fries or rice.

Serves 6
Time 30 minutes

Ham with Pasta
(Zambon Kai Pasta)

4 lbs.	Ham, cubed
3 tbsp.	Butter
1 tsp.	Salt
1/2 tsp.	Pepper
1/4 tsp.	Cinnamon
2	Large Onions, chopped
1 cup	Tomato Paste
2 quarts	Water
2	Cinnamon Sticks
1/2 cup	Grated Parmesan Cheese
1 pckg.	Favorite pasta

Method:

Place cubed ham in a skillet and brown in 1 1/2 tbsp. butter. Add salt, pepper and cinnamon. Add the onions and let soften. Mix in the remaining ingredients and cook for 3 hours or until sauce becomes thick and the meat well done. Cook and drain the pasta as per package directions. Place cooked pasta in serving bowl and top with ham mixture. Mix well and serve.

Serves 10
Time 3 1/2 hours

ROAST LAMB A LA GREQUE
ARNI PSITO, LEMONI

Pork Cutlets in Sauce
(Kotoletes Hirines)

6	Pork Cutlets, lean
1/2 cup	Butter
1/2 cup	Dry Red Wine
2	Medium Onions, chopped
4	Garlic Cloves, chopped
2	Celery Stalks, chopped
1	Green Pepper, chopped
1-14 oz.	Can Tomatoes
1 tsp.	Parsley, chopped
1 tsp.	Salt
1/2 tsp.	Pepper
1/2 tsp.	Oregano
1 cup	Water

Method:

In a skillet, place half of the butter and sauté the onions, celery, garlic, green pepper, oregano, parsley, salt and pepper for 5 minutes. Add the water and simmer for 30 minutes or until mixture is thickened. In another skillet place the remaining butter and fry the pork cutlets well on both sides. Remove to the skillet with the sauce and simmer together for 5 minutes. Serve on top of spaghetti or rice.

Serves 6
Time 1 hour

Greek Pork with Celery
(Selino Me Hirino)

6	Pork Chops, lean
3 tbsp.	Olive Oil
2	Large Onions, chopped
4	Carrots, cut into 2" pieces
3/4 cup	Water
1	Celery Head, cut into 2" pieces

Sauce:
1 tbsp.	Corn Starch
3 tbsp.	Water
2	Eggs, separated
3 tbsp.	Lemon Juice

Method:

Brown the chops in oil, add onions and carrots. Sauté for 5 minutes. Place the celery pieces on top of this mixture and continue cooking for about 20 minutes. Add water as needed. To prepare the sauce, drain the liquid from the meat. Add water or prepared stock to make 1 cup. To this add the cornstarch, diluted in 3 tbsp. water. Cook until liquid is thick and clear. Beat the egg whites until stiff. Add the egg yolks and the lemon juice. Continue beating, then gradually add the hot stock. Pour over the meat and vegetables. Serve with your favorite type of rice, pasta, potatoes and vegetables.

Serves 6
Time 1 1/2 hours

Roast Pork
(Hirino Riganato)

4 lbs.	Pork Loin
1 tsp.	Salt
1/2 tsp.	Pepper
2 lbs.	Large Potatoes
1 tsp.	Oregano
2 cups	Water
2	Lemons, juice only

Method:

Season the meat with salt, pepper, oregano and rub with lemon juice. Preheat the oven to 350 degrees and bake for about 2 hours (allow about 45 minutes per pound). Scoop the potatoes with a melon baller or cut into 1" cubes. Discard any left overs. Place in a plastic bowl, season with salt and pepper and lemon juice. Mix well. When meat is almost done, add the potatoes around the roast and bake for 1 hour, basting and turning frequently.

Serves 8
Time 3 1/2 hours

STUFFED PORK LOIN
(YEMISTO HIRINO)

3 lbs.	Extra Large Potatoes
4 lbs.	Pork Loin, sliced widthwise into 1 piece
2	Onions, finely chopped
2	Celery Stalks, finely chopped
2	Garlic Cloves, minced
1/2 lb.	Fresh Mushrooms, diced
1 tsp.	Salt
1/2 tsp.	Pepper
1 tsp.	Parsley, finely chopped
1/2 tsp.	Oregano
2	Eggs
1/4 cup	Bread Crumbs
1/4 cup	Currants
1/4 cup	Pine Nuts
2 cups	Water
2	Lemons, juice only

Method:

Preheat oven to 350 degrees. Combine all the ingredients except the lemon juice and potatoes. Mix well to form a stiff mixture. Open up the pork loin where it was sliced and place the mixture down the length of meat. Roll up in the same manner you would a jelly roll. Secure with string in 3-4 places. Place the rolled meat in a casserole dish along with 2 cups water and the lemon juices. Cook in oven for 2 hours. Scoop the potatoes with a melon bailer or cube into 1 1/2" cubes. Add to the meat just before the meat is done. Baste often and turn. Remove the roast from the pan and remove the strings. Slice into 1" thick slices and serve.

Serves 8
Time 3 1/2 hours

Greek Sausages
(Loukanika Ellinika)

1 lb.	Ground Beef
1 lb.	Ground Pork
1 tsp.	Orange Rind, grated
20	Black Peppercorns, cracked
1/2 cup	Red Wine
1/2 cup	Lemon Juice
3	Garlic Cloves, minced
1 tsp.	Salt
1 tsp.	Pepper
1 tsp.	Allspice
1 tsp.	Cinnamon
3 doz.	Sausage Casings

Method:

Mix all the ingredients except the lemon juice and casings together in a large bowl. Refrigerate covered for 1 week, stirring daily. Use a proper attachment on a grinder so you can stuff the mixture into casings and separate into 12" lengths. Prick the casings with a fork and string up to dry for 1 week in a cool, dry place. To cook, cut into 1" pieces and broil. Sprinkle with lemon juice and serve hot.

Makes 2 1/2 dozen
Time   1 1/2 hours

Greek Halvah
(Ellinikos Halvas)

1 cup	Unsalted Butter
2 cups	White Sugar
3 cups	Wheatlets
4 cups	Water
1/2 cup	Blanched Almonds

Method:

Place all the sugar in a heavy saucepan along with the water and the blanched almonds (whole). Simmer over a low heat for about 30 minutes. In a separate pan, brown the butter and add the wheatlets. Stir continuously until golden brown. Add the sugar and almond mixture to this slowly. THIS WILL SIZZLE VIOLENTLY, SO DO NOT STAND DIRECTLY OVER THE POT!! Stir continuously until it begins to thicken. Remove from heat and set aside. Drape a clean tea towel across the top of this pan and then place the lid on it. This removes all excess moisture. Let stand for about 10 minutes then pour into molds or into a cake pan. Remove from molds when room temperature and sprinkle with cinnamon.

Serves 15
Time 30 minutes

Honey Cheese Pie
(Tyri Me Meli Pita)

2 cups	Ricotta Cheese
1 cup	Honey
4	Eggs
2 tbsp.	Flour
1 tsp.	Lemon Juice
1 tsp.	Cinnamon

Method:

Beat the eggs lightly in a mixing bowl. Add the cheese, honey, cinnamon, flour and lemon juice and beat until very smooth. Rub 1 tbsp. butter into a 9" pie pan. Pour in the batter. Bake in preheated oven at 350 degrees for 1 hour. Sprinkle with cinnamon, let cool, then cut into wedges.

Serves 8-10
Time 1 1/2 hours

Honey Puffs
(Loukoumathes)

1 cup	Liquid Honey
2	Eggs
3 cups	Flour
3 tsp.	Baking Powder
1 tbsp	Orange Rind, grated
1/2 cup	Currants
	Water, enough to make sticky batter
	Oil, enough for deep frying
	Cinnamon

Method:

Mix all ingredients together except for the honey, oil and cinnamon. Beat well until the batter is bubbly. Drop by the teaspoon into the heated deep fryer. Brown on both sides. Break open to ensure that they are cooked through. Remove from oil and pat on paper towels to absorb some of the oil. Serve hot with liquid honey drizzled over them, then sprinkle with cinnamon. Delicious! These may be served as a dessert or as a breakfast feature.

Serves 6
Time 45 minutes

Honey Cookies
(Melomakarona)

2 1/3 cups	Olive Oil
1 cup	Sugar
4 tsp.	Honey, melted
1/2 tsp.	Salt
1/2 cup	Orange Juice
1 1/2 tsp.	Baking Soda
6 1/2 cups	Flour
1 1/2 tsp.	Cinnamon
1/2 tsp.	Cloves
1/2 tsp.	Nutmeg
1/2 tsp.	Allspice
1/2 tsp.	Baking Powder

Syrup:

1 cup	Sugar
1 cup	Honey
1 cup	Water
1/2 cup	Walnuts, chopped

Method:

Combine the baking soda and the orange juice. Add the oil and stir well. Gradually add the sugar and the melted honey and mix. Combine all the dry ingredients and sift together. Add to the oil mixture gradually, until a firm but moist dough is formed. Knead for about 5 minutes. Form dough into walnut-sized balls. Place on lightly greased cookie sheet and flatten slightly with a fork. Bake at 350 degrees for 20-25 minutes or until golden brown. Make the syrup by combining all the ingredients except for the walnuts in a heavy saucepan. Bring to a boil, then remove from heat. When cookies have cooled, dip into the hot syrup. Sprinkle with crushed walnuts. Continue in this manner until all the cookies are stacked on a tray. Pour any remaining syrup over the stack and let sit overnight, covered. These cookies keep very well as long as they remain covered and moist. Ideal cookie for Christmas.

Makes 3 dozen
Time 1 hour

Greek-Style Grape Pudding
(Moustalevria)

1 quart	White or Red Grape Juice
5 tbsp.	Cornstarch
1/2 cup	Cold Water
	Whipping Cream or Cinnamon
	Sesame Seeds, toasted

Method:

Beat the cornstarch in the cold water until perfectly smooth. Set aside. In a saucepan over low heat, bring the grape juice to a boil. Add the cornstarch mixture to this slowly, stirring constantly for 1 minute. When the pudding begins to boil again, remove from heat and beat with a whisk until slightly cooled. Pour into individual serving dishes. Refrigerate for at least 3 hours. Garnish with whipped cream or cinnamon. Sprinkle with sesame seeds and serve.

Serves 6
Time 20 minutes

Fritter Puffs
(Tiganites)

1 cup	Water
1/4 lb.	Unsalted Butter
1/2 tsp.	Salt
1 tsp.	Granulated Sugar
1 cup	Flour
1/2 tsp.	Baking soda
4	Eggs, room temperature
2 tbsp.	Rum or 1 tbsp. Orange Flavoring
3 cups	Light Vegetable Oil
1 1/2 cups	Icing Sugar

Method:

Combine water, butter, salt and granulated sugar in a small pan. Bring to a boil, stirring constantly. Add the flour and baking soda all at once to this mixture. Continue to cook, stirring vigorously until the batter leaves the sides of the pan. Transfer the batter to a large bowl and add 1 egg at a time, beating well after each egg. Add flavoring and beat on high speed for about 4 minutes. Heat oil in a deep fryer to 375 degrees. Drop batter by teaspoonful into the hot oil. Be sure not to crowd too many in at once. Puffs will turn on their own when one side is brown. Remove and drain on paper towel. Continue to cook until all are done. Stack on platter and sprinkle with icing sugar or liquid honey, or your favorite syrup.

Serves 8-10
Time 1 hour

Mousaka
Mousakas

Easter Plait
(Lambropsomo)

1 cup	Milk
1/4 cup	Butter
1 pkg.	Dry Yeast
1/2 cup	Sugar
1 tsp.	Salt
2	Eggs
3 tbsp.	Orange Juice
1 tsp.	Orange Rind
5 1/2 cups	Flour

Glaze:

2 tbsp.	Sugar
1/4 cup	Slivered Almonds
2 tbsp.	Orange Juice

Method:

Heat milk and butter to scalding point. Pour into large bowl, cool to lukewarm. Sprinkle yeast over milk, add sugar and salt. Lightly mix together. Stir in the beaten eggs, orange juice and rind. Add half the flour and beat until bubbles form. Add remaining flour or just enough to make soft dough. Knead until dough is smooth and elastic. Place in lightly buttered bowl, brush with butter, and let rise until double in size. Punch down and divide dough in half. Divide each half into 3 equal parts. Shape each piece into long strands and braid 3 together. Place plaits in buttered pan large enough to fit and cover. Let rise until doubled in size again. Bake for 20 minutes at 375 degrees.

Glaze

Pour the juice into a small pan and heat up to boiling. Add the sugar, stirring well until all is dissolved. Remove from heat. Brush bread with glaze and sprinkle with almonds throughout the baking time. Remove from oven and cool before cutting.

Makes 2 loaves
Time 3 hours

Custard Pie
(Galatoboureko)

5 cups	Sugar
2 cups	Water
2 tbsp.	Lemon Juice
6 cups	Milk
6	Egg Yolks, room temperature
1 cup	Uncooked Farina or Cream of Wheat
1 tsp.	Vanilla/Orange Extract
1 lb.	Unsalted Butter
1 lb.	Phyllo Pastry, unsalted

Method:

You start this recipe off by preparing a syrup:
Combine 4 cups of the sugar with all the water and lemon juice in a saucepan. Cook over medium heat for 15 minutes. Remove from heat and set aside. Scald milk and keep it warm. Combine the egg yolks and remaining sugar in a large bowl. Beat with whisk for 6 minutes. Add farina or Cream of Wheat and mix well with a wooden spoon. Transfer this mixture to a large pot. Add the vanilla and cook over low heat, stirring constantly to prevent lumping. Cook for 15 minutes or until the mixture is smooth, thick and creamy. Refrigerate. Melt butter in a small

saucepan over very low heat. DO NOT LET IT BROWN! Butter a baking pan 13"x9" and layer the bottom with full sheets of the phyllo, brushing each sheet with butter first. Use 8-10 sheets. Spread out custard on top of this bottom layer of pastry. Lay 8-10 sheets pastry on top of this, each one buttered as you did for the bottom layer. Sprinkle top layer of phyllo with water to prevent it from curling when baking. Bake in preheated 350 degree oven until golden brown and crisp. Pour syrup over pastry, until pastry has absorbed all. Allow to cool in the pan for 4 hours before cutting. Do not cover while cooling. Cut into squares after 4 hours and serve.

Serves 20
Time 2 1/2 hours

Greek Corn Bread
(Bobota)

1 cup	Flour
1 cup	Cornmeal
1 tsp.	Baking Powder
1/4 tsp.	Baking Soda
1/4 cup	Sugar
1/2 tsp	Salt
3 tbsp.	Honey
1/3 cup	Orange Juice
3/4 cup	Warm Water
3 tbsp	Warm Olive Oil
1 tsp.	Orange Rind, grated
1/2 cup	Currants
1/2 cup	Syrup (*see Sweet Greek Syrup)

Method:

Sift all dry ingredients into a large bowl. In a separate bowl, combine the honey, orange juice, water and oil. Stir well. Combine wet with dry ingredients, beating with a wooden spoon until smooth. Fold in the currants and the orange rind. Pour the mixture into a 7"x7" well-greased square pan and bake for 25 minutes in a preheated 375 degree oven. Let cool. Pour warm syrup over it and serve immediately.

Makes 9 pieces
Time 1 hour

Chestnut Fritters
(Tiganites' Kastana)

1 cup	Chestnut Puree, canned
1	Egg Yolk
2 tbsp.	Heavy Cream
1 tsp.	Sugar
1/4 tsp.	Vanilla

Fritter Batter:

1 cup	Flour
1/4 tsp.	Baking Powder
1	Egg
1/4 tsp.	Salt
	Water, enough to make runny batter

Method:

In a bowl, combine all the above ingredients and shape into 3/4" balls. Combine all ingredients for batter in a separate bowl to make a runny batter. Dip into the fritter batter and deep fry at 375 degrees until golden brown. Transfer from oil to a paper towel to drain. Sift icing sugar over the fritters and serve hot.

Serves 4
Time 30 minutes

Christmas Bread
(Cristopsomo)

1/2 cup	Milk
1/4 lb.	Butter
2	Eggs, beaten
3/4 cup	Sugar
1/2 tsp.	Salt
1 tsp.	Vanilla
6 cups	Flour
3 pkgs.	Dry Yeast
1/2 tbsp.	Sugar
1/2 cup	Warm Water

Spice Liquid:

1/2 tsp.	Cinnamon
1/2 tsp.	Orange Peel, grated
2	Bay Leaves
2 tsp.	Vanilla
5 pieces	Mastiha, washed and unground
1/4 cup	Orzo or Brandy
3/4 cup	Water

Method:

Prepare spice liquid first by boiling all ingredients together and simmering for 30 minutes. Set aside. Set yeast by dissolving the sugar in the warm water. Sprinkle yeast into this and let sit until completely foamy. Scald the milk and butter together in a small saucepan. Pour into a large mixing bowl to cool. Add sugar, salt, beaten eggs and vanilla. Stir in 1/2 cup of the spice liquid. Pour in the yeast. Stir well. Add 1/2 the flour and beat until bubbly. Add the remaining flour or enough to make a soft dough. Knead until smooth and elastic. Place in a lightly greased bowl, brush with melted butter and let rise until doubled in size. Punch down and divide in half. Shape into small loaf and place in lightly greased baking pan. Keep a small fistful aside to make Byzantine cross. Roll out small strips from what you kept aside and press into crosses. Place in the middle of the top of each loaf. Decorate the middle of each with cherries or walnuts. Let rise and bake at 375 degrees for about 30 minutes. Bread is done when it sounds hollow when tapped.

Makes 2 loaves
Time 1 1/2 hours

BLACK CHERRY PRESERVE
(MAVRO KERRASI)

3 lbs.	Black Cherries, pitted
6 cups	Sugar
1 1/2 cups	Water
1 1/2	Lemons, juice only

Method:

Wash and pit the cherries and place in a heavy saucepan along with the sugar. Add water to the cherries and let stand for 1 hour before simmering for 30 minutes. Stir occasionally and skim any scum that forms while cooking. Cook until jelly stage. Add the lemon juice to prevent crystallization. Pour into sterilized and ready jars. Let cool at room temperature before storing.

Time 1 hour

BUTTER COOKIES
(KOURAMBIEDES)

2 cups	Sugar
6	Eggs
9 cups	Flour
1 lb.	Unsalted Butter
1 tsp.	Vanilla
2 tbsp.	Baking Powder
1 tbsp.	Water
1	Egg

Method:

Cream butter and beat in the sugar and eggs until light and creamy. Sift together the flour and baking powder. Slowly blend into the butter mixture to make a soft dough. With floured hands, shape the dough into desired shapes (crescents, balls flattened with fork, etc.) and place on cookie sheet. Brush cookies with beaten egg and water. Bake in preheated 375 degree oven for 20 minutes.

Makes 8 dozen
Time 1 hour

Greek Coffee Biscuits
(Biscotta Caffe)

6	Eggs
12 cups	Flour
1 tsp.	Vanilla
1 cup	Walnuts, chopped
1 cup	Olive Oil
2 cups	Sugar
2 tsp.	Baking Powder

Method:

Place all ingredients except for flour into a large bowl. Gradually add the flour until you have a stiff dough that can be handled and shaped easily. Shape into small loaves 1" in height and 8" long. Place on baking sheet and bake in preheated 350 degree oven for about 30 minutes. Remove loaves and slice diagonally into slices. Lay the slices on their sides back in the baking pan. Bake again for 30 minutes. Remove, and when cool store in airtight jar. These are very similar to Italian biscotti.

Makes 14 dozen
Time 1 hour

Lamb with Cauliflower
(Arni Me Kounoupithi Stifatho)

4 lbs.	Boneless Lamb Meat
3	Medium Cauliflower Heads
1/4 cup	Olive Oil
16	Small Onions
4	Garlic Cloves, cut in half
2 tbsp.	Tomato Paste, diluted in 2 cups water
1 cup	Red Wine Vinegar
1/2 tbsp.	Rosemary
2	Bay Leaves
12	Peppercorns

Method:

Cut the lamb into 1 1/2" cubes and sauté in a casserole dish with 4 tbsp. oil until brown. Break the cauliflower into flowerettes. In a separate skillet sauté the cauliflower, small whole onions and garlic halves until brown. Add 4 cups water to the meat and simmer on a medium heat for about 1 1/2 hours, or until tender. Add the tomato paste diluted in 2 cups water, vinegar, rosemary, bay leaf, vegetable mixture and cook for about 30 minutes. Cover and let simmer.

Serves 8
Time 2 1/2 hours

Baklava

1/2 lb.	Almonds, ground
1/2 lb.	Walnuts, ground
1/2 cup	Sugar
2 tsp.	Cinnamon, ground
1/2 tsp.	Cloves, ground
1 lb.	Unsalted Butter
1 lb.	Phyllo Pastry

Syrup:

2 cups	Sugar
2 cups	Water
1/2	Cinnamon Stick
1 1/2 tbsp.	Honey
1/2	Lemon, juice only

Method:

To make the syrup, combine the sugar, water and cinnamon in a saucepan. Bring to a boil and simmer for 30 minutes. Add honey and lemon juice, boil a few minutes longer, remove from heat and set aside. Mix the almonds, walnuts, sugar, cinnamon and ground cloves together thoroughly. In a 9"x13" baking pan lightly buttered, place buttered sheets of phyllo, folded to fit the pan, using no more than 3 sheets per phyllo layer. Layer this with a generous heap of the nut mixture. Relayer with buttered phyllo, continuing, but being sure that the middle layers do not contain more than 3 layers of nuts. Finish with the top layer of phyllo. Brush with butter. With a sharp knife, cut the baklava in lengthwise rows, evenly. In the center of each row, place whole cloves about 2" apart. Pour remainder of melted butter over the top evenly. Bake in preheated oven at 350 degrees for 30 minutes. Lower temperature to 300 degrees and continue to bake for additional 45 minutes, or until evenly browned. Remove from oven and pour cooled syrup over the baklava, cover and let cool. It is best served the next day. Cut into squares with a clove in each piece.

Serves 8-12
Time 2 hours

Chicken Liver Pate
(Kotopoulo Sikoti)

3 cups	Chicken Livers, chopped
2	Medium Onions
1 cup	Mayonnaise
1/4 cup	Cognac (optional)
2	Hard Boiled Eggs
1 tsp.	Salt
1/2 tsp.	Pepper

Method:

Boil the chicken livers in a pot of water for 15 minutes. Drain and let cool. Chop finely. Place into a blender together with the mayonnaise, onion, cognac, eggs, salt and pepper. Beat until fluffy. Pour into a greased 3 cup mold and refrigerate overnight. Remove from mold by placing a hot wet towel around the mold to loosen the pate. Serve immediately with cheeses and dry bread or crackers.

Serves 12
Time 45 minutes

Fried Cheese
(Saganaki)

1/2 lb.	Kasseri, Kefalotiri, or Fresh Whole Parmesan Cheese
1/2 cup	Flour
1/4 lb.	Butter
2 1/2 tbsp.	Lemon Juice
1/4 tsp.	Oregano

Method:

Cut desired cheese into slices about 1/2" thick. Set aside. Heat butter in heavy frying pan until very hot. Dust cheese lightly with flour and fry in hot butter for about 30 seconds per side. Sprinkle with lemon juice and oregano and serve immediately. This makes a wonderful appetizer for meat dishes and is easily a favorite among cheese lovers.

Serves 4
Time 10 minutes

Fried Mushrooms
(Manitaria Tiganita)

1 lb.	Fresh Whole Mushrooms
1 tsp.	Salt
1/2 tsp.	Pepper
1/4 tsp.	Flour
1/2 cup	Olive Oil
1	Lemon, juice only

Method:

In a heavy skillet, preheat oil over medium heat. Clean, rinse and trim mushrooms. Coat with salt and pepper. Roll in flour, being sure to coat well. Drop into hot oil, turning constantly, until golden brown. Remove and let drain on paper towel or in strainer. Sprinkle with lemon juice and serve hot.

Serves 4
Time 20 minutes

Feta Dip
(Feta Alima)

1 lb.	Fresh Feta Cheese
1/4 cup	Olive Oil
1 cup	Milk
1 1/2 cups	Walnuts, chopped
1 tsp.	Paprika
1/4 tsp.	Cayenne Pepper

Method:

Place half of the feta cheese (broken into pieces) into the blender, along with half the milk, oil and walnuts. Blend until smooth. Pour into a bowl and set aside. Repeat with the other half of the ingredients. Pour into the bowl along with the first half, add the cayenne pepper and mix well. Refrigerate until firm. Sprinkle with paprika and serve.

Makes 4 cups
Time 30 minutes

Squid Rings
(Kalamarakia Rotheles)

1 lb.	Fresh Squid Tubes (available frozen or fresh from most grocers or seafood suppliers)
2	Eggs
1 tsp.	Wine Vinegar
1 tsp.	Salt
1 tsp.	Pepper
1 cup	Flour
1 cup	Olive Oil
1 cup	Tartar Sauce or Tzatziki Sauce (or your favorite seafood sauce)
1	Lemon, juice only

Method:

Wash and clean squid tubes well. This entails removing the head, pulling out the cartilage of the spine and squeezing and flushing out all ink. Some may also contain a rubbery ball of eggs, which should be disposed of too. This can be quite a messy job, so be sure to do this in the sink. Cut the body into strips width wise to make uniform rings about 1/4" wide. Place the meat in a sieve to drain. Break the eggs into a large bowl and add the salt, pepper, vinegar and oil. Beat together well. Add the squid rings to the mixture and let stand for 5 minutes. Remove the rings and place into the flour, coating thoroughly. Heat enough oil in a heavy skillet to cover the bottom of the pan. Place in the coated squid and let fry over medium heat until golden brown. Remove from heat. Place on serving platter and sprinkle with lemon juice and parsley. This dish can be served with a salad or french fries, or by itself with tzatziki sauce as a delicious appetizer.

Serves 6
Time 25 minutes

Salmon Roe Dip
(Avga Solomou)

1-7 oz.	Jar Salmon Roe
1/2 lb.	Feta Cheese
1/2 lb.	Sour Cream
1 cup	Walnuts, chopped
2 tbsp.	Mayonnaise
1/4 tsp.	Cayenne Pepper
1 tsp.	Paprika

Method:

Crumble the feta together with the walnuts, mayonnaise and sour cream into a blender. Blend until smooth. Pour mixture into a large bowl. Fold in the cayenne pepper and salmon roe. Refrigerate. Sprinkle with paprika before serving.

Makes 2 1/2 cups
Time 30 minutes

Snail Stew
(Saligaria Stifatho)

2-12 oz.	Cans Escargot
3	Large Onions, sliced
1 cup	Olive Oil
2	Garlic Cloves, minced
1/2 cup	Red Wine
2 lbs.	Ripe Tomatoes, chopped
1	Bay Leaf
1 tsp.	Salt
1/2 tsp.	Pepper

Method:

Preheat oil in a heavy skillet and sauté the onions. Add minced garlic, wine and tomatoes and let simmer for 15 minutes. Place bay leaf into mixture and salt and pepper to taste. Add the escargot, cover and simmer for about 30 minutes. Uncover after this time and allow to simmer until all liquid is absorbed. Serve with rice or your favorite style of potatoes. (If fresh snails are used, increase the cooking time by 15 minutes.)

Serves 6
Time 1 hour

Fried Oysters
(Strithia Tiganita)

2 quarts	Large oysters, cleaned
2	Eggs, slightly beaten
1 tsp.	Salt
1/2 tsp.	Pepper
1/2 cup	Flour
1/2 cup	Olive Oil
1	Lemon

Method:

Sift together dry ingredients. Beat eggs and add to flour mixture to produce a thick batter. Place oysters in the mixture and let stand. Heat oil in a heavy skillet over medium heat. Spoon out 1 oyster at a time from batter and drop into hot oil. Fry until golden brown on both sides. Serve with lemon or tartar sauce.

Serves 6
Time 20 minutes

Spinach Cheese Puffs
(Spanakopites)

2-10 oz.	Packages Frozen Spinach (or 2 lbs. fresh)
6 tbsp.	Olive Oil
6	Green Onions, minced
1 lb.	Feta Cheese
12 oz.	Dry Cottage Cheese
1/2 cup	Fresh Parsley, finely chopped
1/4 tsp.	White Pepper
1 tsp.	Dill
6	Eggs, room temperature, well beaten
1/2 lb.	Unsalted Butter
1 lb.	Phyllo Pastry, room temperature

Method:

Thaw frozen spinach (about 2 hours). If using fresh spinach, wash well, drain and chop into fine pieces. Heat oil over medium heat in skillet and sauté onions until soft. Remove from heat and set aside. Add spinach and simmer until moisture evaporates. Rinse feta cheese under cold water, drain and crumble into a bowl. Blend in cottage cheese, parsley, dill and pepper. Add beaten eggs and mix well. Stir in onions and spinach. Gently unfold phyllo pastry. Using sharp, clean scissors, gently cut the phyllo stack into 3 equal lengthwise strips. Wrap 2 of the 3 stacks in plastic and refrigerate until needed. Cover remaining stack with damp towel and work with 1 sheet at a time. Take first strip and gently fold both long sides in toward the middle of the strip. Brush with melted butter to keep from drying out. Place 1 tsp. spinach-cheese mixture into the bottom left corner of the pastry strip. Fold this corner over so the bottom edge touches the right or left edge of the strip, forming a right-angle triangle. Continue in this manner until entire strip is folded to form a multi-layered triangle. Continue with remaining strips until everything is complete. Place on baking sheet, being sure not to let triangles touch. Brush again with melted butter and bake in preheated oven at 425 degrees until crisp and golden brown (about 12-15 minutes).

Serves 12-15
Time 3 1/2 hours

FISH ROE SALAD
(TARAMOSALATA)

4 oz	Fish Roe
4	Slices Dry Bread
1	Small Onion, finely grated
1 tsp.	Dill, chopped
1 cup	Olive Oil
1/4 cup	Lemon Juice

Method:

Soak fish roe in water for a few minutes, then drain. Trim crusts from bread. Place in a bowl of water and let soak for 3 minutes. Remove bread and squeeze out excess moisture. Place all ingredients into a blender or mixer and blend on low speed until light and creamy. Refrigerate until ready to serve. Serve on melba toast or other cracker, or fresh bread.

Serves 10
Time 30 minutes

Bean Salad
(Fasolia Salata)

1 lb.	Navy White Beans
1	Medium Onion, diced
1/2 tsp.	Fresh Parsley, finely chopped
6 tbsp.	Olive Oil
2 tbsp.	Wine Vinegar
1/2 tsp.	Salt
1/2 tsp.	Oregano
1/2 tsp.	Pepper

Method:

Wash beans well, place in pot, cover with cold water and let soak overnight. Boil until tender the next day. Drain the beans and place into a bowl along with the parsley, oregano and onions. Toss well. In a smaller bowl beat together salt, pepper, oil and vinegar. Pour over salad and toss well. Refrigerate for 2 hours before serving.

Serves 6
Time 1 1/2 hours

Chick Pea Salad
(Revithia Salata)

1 lb.	Chick Peas
1	Medium Onion, chopped
1 tsp.	Parsley, finely chopped
1 tsp.	Oregano
1/4 tsp.	Salt
1/4 tsp.	Pepper
6 tbsp.	Olive Oil
2 tbsp.	Wine Vinegar

Method:

Wash chick peas well before soaking them in cold water overnight. Change the water the next day, add salt and boil them until tender, about 1 hour. Drain and place in bowl. Add finely chopped onions, parsley, oregano and stir well. In a separate bowl, beat together the vinegar, salt and pepper. Pour over the pea mixture and toss. Refrigerate until ready to serve.

Serves 6
Time 1 1/2 hours

Chicken a L'orange
Kotopoulo, Portokali

Chick Peas with Salmon
(Revithia Me Solomo)

1-7 oz.	Can Salmon
4	Green Onion, minced
1 tbsp	Parsley, minced
1 tbsp.	Celery, minced
1-20 oz.	Can Chick Peas

Dressing:

1	Garlic Clove, crushed
1/4 tsp.	English Hot Mustard
1/2 tsp.	Salt
1/4 tsp.	Pepper
1/2 cup	Olive Oil
4 tbsp.	Lemon Juice
1/2 tbsp.	Oregano
1/2 tbsp.	Marjoram

Method:

Drain the liquid from the salmon and the peas. Toss together into a bowl. Mix in chopped vegetables and set aside. Place all spices for dressing, lemon juice and mustard into a container with a tight-fitting lid. Cover tightly and shake to mix. Pour the dressing over the vegetables and serve.

Serves 6
Time 15 minutes

Country Salad
(Horiatiki Salata)

3	Tomatoes, cut into wedges
1/2	Small Cucumber
1/2	Large Green Pepper
1/2	Small Onion
1/4 lb.	Feta Cheese
1 doz.	Black Olives

Dressing:

1/2 tsp.	Dried Oregano
6 tbsp.	Olive Oil
2 tbsp.	Wine Vinegar
	Salt and Pepper to taste

Method:

Cut tomatoes into wedges. Dice the cucumber, onion and green pepper. Place into a large bowl. Pit the olives if not already done and add to the mixture in the bowl. Stir. Combine the oil, vinegar, oregano, salt and pepper into a smaller bowl and whisk together briefly. Pour over vegetable mixture and toss lightly. Top with crumbled feta cheese.

Serves 4
Time   15 minutes

Greek Salad
(Salata Eliniki)

4	Stalks Bibb Lettuce
4	Medium Tomatoes
2	Cucumbers, peeled and sliced
2	Medium Green Peppers
1/4 lb.	Feta Cheese
16	Pitted Black Olives
2 tbsp.	Wine Vinegar
1/2 tsp.	Salt
1/4 tsp.	Pepper
1 tbsp.	Fresh Parsley, chopped

Method:

Separate the leaves from 4 stalks of bibb lettuce. Rinse and pat dry. Line a large bowl with the leaves, add tomato wedges, cucumber slices, crumbled feta, pitted olives and green peppers. Combine oil and spices, mix well and pour over the vegetables. Salt and pepper to taste. Toss and garnish with fresh parsley.

Serves 6
Time 20 minutes

LENTIL AND ANCHOVIE SALAD
(FAKI ME PASTI SARTHELA SALATA)

1 cup	Lentils
4 cups	Water
1/2 cup	Dill Pickles, diced
1/4 cup	Green Onions, chopped
8	Anchovie Fillets, chopped
3 tbsp.	Capers, minced
2 tbsp.	Parsley
1/4 cup	Tarragon Vinegar
1/2 cup	Olive Oil
1/2 tsp.	Salt
1/4 tsp.	Pepper

Method:

Rinse the lentils and place in a large saucepan with 4 cups salted water. Bring to a boil. Reduce heat and simmer covered for about 30 minutes. Drain and transfer to a bowl and let cool. Add to this the dill pickles, green onions, anchovie fillets, drained capers and parsley. Set aside. In another bowl, beat the tarragon vinegar, salt and olive oil gradually. Toss lentil mixture with the dressing and chill covered for about 2 hours. Garnish with slices of hard boiled eggs.

Serves 6
Time   1 hour

Vegetable Salad
(Salata Eliniki Me Horta)

1 lb.	Carrots
1 lb.	Cauliflower
3	Medium Eggplants
1/2 lb.	Green Beans
1/2 lb.	Mushroom Buttons
1	Jar Anchovies
1	Jar Pimentos
	Marinade (Refer to marinade recipe in the sauce section of this book.)

Method:

Peel the carrots, trimming the ends and cut into sticks. Separate the cauliflower into small flowerettes. Slice the eggplant into 1/3" slices. Set all these aside. Boil the green beans for about 8 minutes, or until tender. Set aside. In a heavy saucepan, simmer each vegetable separately in the marinade for about 8 minutes. Return all vegetables to the marinade and let cool. Place in refrigerator to chill. Add lemon juice and salt to taste. Arrange the vegetables on a platter and drizzle with the marinade. Serve at room temperature or chilled and with a serving of pita bread.

Serves 6
Time   1 hour

Zucchini Salad
(Kolokithaki Salata)

1 lb.	Zucchini
4	Tomatoes, cut into wedges
1	Green Bell Pepper, cut into strips
1/2 cup	Green Onions, chopped
1/2 cup	Parsley, fresh and diced

Dressing:

3/4 cup	Olive Oil
1/4 cup	Wine Vinegar
4	Garlic Cloves
1/2 tsp.	Salt
Dash	Pepper

Method:

Boil zucchini in small pot for about 10 minutes. Drain. Cut into thin slices. Combine with the tomatoes, green peppers, onions and parsley in a bowl. In a smaller bowl, beat together the oil, vinegar, salt, pepper and minced garlic. Pour over the salad, toss and refrigerate for at least 2 hours.

Serves 8
Time 20 minutes

Bean Soup
(Soupa Palasoli)

1 lb.	Navy Beans
4	Carrots, medium
4	Celery Sticks
1	Medium Onion
1/2 cup	Olive Oil
2 qrts.	Water
4	Sprigs Parsley
3	Bay Leaves
1 tsp.	Salt
1/2 tsp.	Black Pepper

Method:

Wash and drain the beans well. Place them in a deep dutch oven or casserole dish. Cover them in plenty of water and soak overnight. Drain and rinse well the next day. Re-cover with the same amount of fresh water. Add salt, pepper, bay leaves and place over medium heat for about 2 hours to simmer. The skin will begin to flake off the beans when they are ready. Finely chop the parsley and onions and add to the beans. Slice the carrots and celery into thin roundels. Place them into the soup with the oil and remaining water. Boil mixture until beans can be pierced easily.

This makes a clear broth soup. If you prefer tomatoes, just add 2 tbsp. of tomato paste to the broth. You may need to increase your spices added initially.

Serves 8
Time 3 hours

GREEK-STYLE CHICKEN AND SOUP
(KOTOPOULO SOUPA AVGOLEMONO)

1	Whole Frying Chicken (4 lbs.)
1	Large Onion, finely chopped
4	Stalks Celery, coarsely chopped
2	Large Carrots, sliced into rounds
4	Eggs
2 quarts	Water
1 pckg.	Spaghetti or Angel Hair Pasta
2	Lemons, juice only
1 tbsp.	Salt
1/2 tbsp.	Pepper
1 tsp.	Parsley

Method:

Wash chicken well and place in a dutch oven or deep casserole dish along with 2 quarts water, salt and pepper, celery, onions and carrots. Boil for about an hour or until tender. Remove the chicken and cut into pieces. Set aside. Beat 4 eggs together well in a bowl. Continue to beat while slowly adding the lemon juice. Beat constantly while adding a cup of the broth from the chicken slowly too. Place the casserole containing the broth and vegetables on the burner, with just enough heat to keep it simmering. Add the lemon-egg mixture to this pot slowly, being sure to whisk or stir as you do. You will find that the soup will thicken quickly from this point on. Remove from heat, add chicken pieces and allow the heat to warm the meat. Prepare pasta as per package instructions.

Serves 6
Time 2 hours

Turkish Delight
Loukoumi

Cucumber Soup
(Soupa Angouri)

3 cups	Grated Cucumber
1 1/2 cups	Cold Water
6 cups	Plain Yogurt
2 tbsp.	Minced Dill
1 tsp.	Salt
1/2 tsp.	Pepper
1	Garlic Clove, minced

Method:

Place ingredients all together into a blender. Blend well. Pour into bowls and chill. Serve with warm garlic bread.

Serves 8
Time 15 minutes

Lamb Soup with Egg and Lemon
(Soupa Arni Avgolemono)

3 lbs.	Lamb Shoulder Meat, cubed
2 lbs.	Lamb Bones (ask your butcher; he may be able to supply you with some)
1/4 cup	Olive Oil
2	Celery Stalks, diced
1	Large Onion, diced
2	Large Carrots, diced
10 cups	Water
2 tsp.	Rosemary
1 tsp.	Thyme
1	Bay Leaf
8	Peppercorns
6	Sprigs Fresh Parsley
5	Eggs
1/2 cup	Lemon Juice
1/2 cup	Heavy Cream
1/2 cup	Orzo
1 tsp.	Salt
1 tsp.	Pepper
	Fresh Dill

Method:

Place meat in heavy saucepan with oil and brown lightly over low heat. Add the celery, onions and carrots, and cook for 5 minutes. Add the water. Tie the rosemary, thyme, bay leaf, peppercorns and parsley into a cheesecloth bag. Place into soup mixture. Add lamb bones to the soup. Simmer covered for about 2 hours, or until the lamb is tender. Skim the froth off the top of soup as it rises. Strain the soup stock into a heavy saucepan, being sure to press all excess liquid from the vegetables. Discard the bones and vegetables. Remove the lamb and set aside. Chill the stock to remove the fat (overnight is best). Next day, bring to a boil again and add the lamb meat and orzo. Cook covered for 15 minutes. In a separate bowl, beat eggs until well beaten, adding the lemon juice a little at a time, beating constantly. Add 1 cup of the hot broth in the same manner. Add this egg-broth mixture into the soup along with fresh dill pieces. Season to taste with salt and pepper. Serve hot.

Serves 6
Time 3 hours collectively

Lentils Puree
(Faki Poure)

1 1/2 cups	Lentils
4 cups	Chicken Stock
1	Medium Onion
2	Cloves
2	Garlic Cloves
1	Stalk Celery
2	Sprigs Fresh Thyme
6	Sprigs Fresh Parsley
1	Bay Leaf
6 tbsp.	Butter

Method:

In a saucepan, combine lentils with chicken stock. Pierce the whole onion with the 2 cloves and place in saucepan. Prepare a bouquet garni, consisting of 1 stalk of celery halved, the sprigs of parsley and thyme, and the bay leaf. Tie together tightly with thread and add to saucepan. Add garlic cloves to saucepan, slightly broken open. Bring mixture to boil over high heat. Reduce heat and cover, allowing to simmer until lentils are soft. Drain the lentils through a sieve, reserving the liquid. Remove and discard the onion, bouquet garni, and the garlic. Put the lentils through the medium disc of a food processor, or blend in a blender to puree. Place back into saucepan. Add 1/2 cup of the reserved liquid, the butter, salt and pepper, and cook the puree over moderate heat, stirring and adding more of the reserved liquid, to keep moist, until hot. This should be thick, like pea soup.

Serves 4
Time 1 hour

GARDEN LENTIL SOUP
(FAKI SOUPA)

3	Medium Carrots, cut into rounds
1	Medium Onion, chopped fine
2	Garlic Cloves, minced
3	Celery Sticks, chopped fine
1/4 cup	Red Wine Vinegar
1 lb.	Lentils
1/2 cup	Olive Oil
1 tsp.	Oregano
1 tsp.	Salt
1 tsp.	Pepper
2	Bay Leaves

Method:

Place lentils in 4 quarts of water in a deep saucepan and let soak overnight. Next day, strain and rinse lentils well. Cover with 4 quarts fresh water in saucepan. Add the salt, pepper, oregano and oil. Cook over medium heat for about 1 hour, or until lentils are soft. Add carrots, onions, celery, garlic and bay leaves. Cover and simmer for another 15 minutes. When carrots are tender, remove from heat and serve into bowls. Add 1 tsp. of red wine vinegar to each bowl. Mix well and serve. This soup is complemented well with a variety of greek olives, feta cheese and fresh French bread or baguettes.

Serves 6
Time 2 hours

GREEK TAHINI SOUP
(TAHINOSOUPA)

1-8 oz	Jar Tahini
1 1/4 cups	Rice
3/4 cup	Cold Water
1/4 cup	Tomato Paste
1 tsp.	Salt
1/4 tsp.	Pepper
2	Lemons, juice only

Method:

Cook the rice in salted water for about 20 minutes. Place tahini in a bowl with 1/2 cup cold water. Add the lemon juice and mix. Combine 1 cup of the rice water slowly into the tahini mixture and blend well. Remove rice from heat and pour the rest of the tahini into it. Add tomato paste. Serve.

Serves 8
Time 45 minutes

Greek-style Braised Artichokes
(Aginares Me Lathi)

2-10 oz.	Pkgs. Frozen Artichoke Hearts
4	Scallions, chopped
1 tbsp.	Dill, minced
1 cup	Water
1/4 cup	Olive Oil
1/4 tsp.	Salt
1/8 tsp.	Pepper
1 tbsp.	Lemon Juice

Method:

Sauté the scallions and dill in the oil. Add the artichoke hearts and sauté for 3 minutes. Add salt, pepper, water and lemon juice. Simmer for 25 minutes. Serve hot. Good served with orzo or rice, or your favorite linguini.

Serves 8
Time 45 minutes

GREEK HALVAH
HALVAS

BAKED ARTICHOKE HALVES
(AGINARES ELLINIKES)

6	Large Artichokes
4 cups	Water
3	Lemons
2	Medium Onions, chopped
1 tbsp.	Flour
1 cup	Olive Oil
1 tsp.	Salt
1/2 tsp.	Pepper

Method:

Cut the stems off artichokes. Remove bottom leaves and with a pair of scissors trim off the brown thorny tips of all remaining leaves. Remove tops and cut each artichoke in half lengthwise. Soak in 3 3/4 cup of water and the juice of 2 lemons. Set aside. Preheat olive oil in a skillet and sauté the onions, sprinkling with flour. Cook until lightly browned. Transfer to roasting pan or casserole dish. Arrange artichokes, cut sides up, in the same pan. Add remaining water, cover and simmer over low heat for 35-40 minutes or until artichokes are tender. Serve warm or cold.

Serves 6
Time 1 1/2 hours

Lentils and Greens
(Soupa Me Prasina)

1 cup	Lentils
2 1/2 cups	Water
2 cups	Zucchini, cubed
1 cup	Leeks, sliced thick
1 cup	Spinach, chopped
2	Celery Stalks, chopped
2	Garlic Cloves
1/4 lb.	Butter
1/2 tsp.	Salt
1/4 tsp.	Pepper

Method:

Place lentils into a saucepan with salted water and bring to a boil. Reduce heat and simmer covered for 30 minutes. Drain in a sieve, reserving 2 tbsp. of the liquid. Preheat butter in a skillet and sauté the zucchini, leeks, spinach, celery and garlic until the vegetables are soft. Add salt and pepper to taste. Place a buttered sheet of waxed paper under the lid and continue cooking for 10 minutes. Add the lentils and reserved liquid stir for 3 minutes. Serve hot.

Serves 4
Time 1 hour

BAKED POTATOES IN TOMATO SAUCE
(PATATES DOMATA)

6	Large Potatoes, long
1	Small Onion, chopped fine
1-19 oz.	Can Crushed Tomatoes
1 tsp.	Parsley, chopped
1 tsp.	Salt
1 tsp.	Pepper
1 tsp.	Oregano
1/4 cup	Olive Oil
1/2 lb.	Mozzarella, shredded

Method:

Peel potatoes and clean well. Slice them about 1/4" thin. Fry these until slightly gold but not too dark. Set aside. Preheat the olive or salad oil. Combine the onions, garlic, parsley and oregano into oil and let cook for a few minutes. Add crushed tomatoes and simmer for about 25 minutes. In a 9"x9" baking pan place your fried potatoes in an even layer to cover the bottom of the pan. Pour the tomato mixture over the potatoes evenly, alternating with the mozzarella cheese. Repeat layering, ending with mozzarella cheese on top. Bake in preheated 375 degree oven for 30 minutes.

Serves 6
Time 1 1/4 hours

Black-Eyed Beans Casserole
(Phasolia Katsarola)

2 cups	Black-Eyed Beans
8 cups	Water
1/2 cup	Olive Oil
1	Large Onion, chopped
1	Large Green Pepper, chopped
1	Large Potato, diced
2 tbsp.	Honey
2 tbsp.	Red Wine Vinegar
2 tbsp.	Parsley, chopped
1 tsp.	Salt
1/2 tsp.	Pepper

Method:

Wash and drain the beans. Place them in a large pot with the water and oil. Simmer for 30 minutes. In a skillet, heat the oil and sauté the onions, green peppers and potato. Add to the beans and simmer until the beans are tender. Add the parsley, honey, vinegar, salt and pepper and continue to simmer for about 10 minutes. Serve hot or cold with olives and feta cheese.

Serves 8
Time 1 hour

Eggplant Sauce
(Melitzana Saltsa)

2 cups	Eggplant, chopped
1-14 oz.	Can Crushed Tomatoes
1/4 lb.	Butter
1	Medium Onion, chopped
1	Garlic Clove, minced
1/2 tsp.	Oregano
1/2 tsp.	Salt
1/2 tsp.	Pepper
1 tsp.	Sugar
1/2 cup	Water

Method:

Preheat butter in a skillet. Sauté the egg plant, garlic and onion for about 5 minutes. Add the tomato mixture, oregano, salt, pepper, sugar and water. Simmer uncovered for about 30 minutes. Add more water if needed. Stir frequently.

Makes 2 cups
Time 1 hour

Fava Beans in Tomato Sauce
(Koukia Saltsa)

2-20 oz.	Cans Broad Beans
1/2 cup	Olive Oil
2	Large Onions, chopped
6	Celery Stalks, chopped
4	Cloves Garlic, minced
1-14 oz.	Can Tomato Sauce
1 cup	Water
1 cup	Red Wine
1 tsp.	Salt
1/2 tsp.	Pepper

Method:

In a large pot heat the oil and sauté the onions and celery. Do not let them brown. Season with garlic and sauté for 2 more minutes. Add the tomato sauce, water and wine, and let cook for 10 minutes. Wash and drain the broad beans and combine with the mixture. Salt and pepper to taste and simmer for 5 more minutes.

Serves 6
Time 45 minutes

Baklava
Baklavas

Potatoes Oregano
(Patates Oregano)

8	Large Potatoes
6 tbsp.	Olive Oil
3 tbsp.	Lemon Juice
1 tsp.	Oregano
1 tsp.	Salt
1/2 tsp.	Pepper

Method:

Clean and peel potatoes. Cover with water and boil for about 25 minutes, or until tender. Drain and cool to room temperature. Remove peel and slice into 1/4" slices. Place in a 1 quart baking dish. Combine olive oil, lemon juice, oregano, salt and pepper together and mix thoroughly. Pour over potatoes and bake in preheated 350 degree oven for 20 minutes.

Serves 8
Time 45 minutes

Potato Musaka
(Patates Mousaka)

4 tbsp.	Olive Oil
1 1/2 lbs.	Potatoes
1	Large Onion, chopped
2 lbs.	Ground Lamb or Beef
1 tbsp.	Oregano
2 tbsp.	Tomato Paste
1 tsp.	Worcestershire Sauce
2	Large Garlic Cloves, chopped
1 tsp.	Salt
1/2 tsp.	Pepper
4 tbsp.	Parmesan Cheese, grated

Sauce:

2 tbsp.	Butter
2 tbsp.	Flour
1 1/4 cup	Milk
1	Egg, lightly beaten
1/2 tsp.	Salt
1/4 tsp.	Pepper

Method:

Heat 3 tbsp. of the oil in a frying pan and fry the potatoes until golden brown. Heat the remaining oil and sauté the onion. Add to this the meat, oregano, tomato paste, Worcestershire sauce, garlic, salt and pepper and cook over medium-low heat for 15 minutes, stirring occasionally. Line a 9"x9"x2" baking dish with most of the potatoes. Cover with half the meat and layer this with the remaining potatoes. Layer remaining meat over this and top with parmesan cheese. Melt butter in a saucepan. Blend in flour and cook for 1 minute over medium-high heat. Add milk gradually, stirring until sauce is thick. Remove from heat. Add egg and season with salt and pepper. Pour sauce over contents of casserole and cover. Bake in preheated oven at 350 degrees for 45 minutes.

Serves 8
Time 1 1/2 hours

POTATOES AND GARLIC
(SKORTHALIA)

2 cups	Olive Oil
1/4 cup	Dry Red Wine
1	Medium Garlic Cluster, crushed
6	Medium Potatoes

Method:

Boil and mash the potatoes. Place in mixer or food processor along with remaining ingredients. Mix well, being sure to scrape sides of bowl periodically. When mixture is thick and creamy, taste for sharpness. The garlic and vinegar tastes should dominate. Adjust to taste. Oil will make it smoother if it is too sharp, and vinegar will do the opposite. Place in a bowl and refrigerate before serving.

Serves 6
Time 1 hour

TOMATOES AND ZUCCHINI
(KOLOKITHIA ME DOMATES)

4	Large Zucchini, sliced
1/4 cup	Olive Oil
1/2 cup	Shallots, minced
2	Garlic Cloves, minced
1 1/2 lbs.	Ripe Tomatoes, peeled, seeded and chopped
2 tbsp.	Lemon Juice
1/2 tsp.	Chervil, minced
1/2 tsp.	Sugar
1/2 tsp.	Salt
1/4 tsp.	Pepper
1	Lemon, seeded and chopped
1/2 tsp.	Tarragon

Method:

In a skillet, sauté the zucchini in the olive oil, adding more oil as needed to prevent sticking. Lightly brown on both sides. Add minced shallots and garlic cloves, sauteing until the shallots are soft. Add tomatoes, lemon juice, chervil, tarragon and sugar. Salt and pepper to taste. Cook the mixture covered over medium heat for 10 minutes. Remove the lid and continue cooking for 20 minutes, stirring occasionally. Once the vegetables are tender and most of the liquid has evaporated, add the lemon. Let the mixture cool covered overnight. Next day, stir and salt and pepper to taste. Transfer to a bowl lined with lettuce leaves and sprinkle with minced fresh basil/parsley.

Serves 4
Time 1 hour

Stuffed Tomatoes
(Domates Yemistes)

16	Medium Tomatoes, well rounded
8	Green Onions
4	Garlic Cloves
1/2 cup	Olive Oil
1 tsp.	Parsley
1 lb.	Ground Beef (optional)
1 tsp.	Salt
1/4 tsp.	Pepper
2 cups	Long Grain Rice

Method:

Cut the tops of the tomatoes off about 3/4 of the way through, making a hinged lid. Scoop out the pulp and seeds, being sure not to puncture the walls of the tomato. Place seeds and pulp in a bowl to the side. Place hollowed tomatoes in baking pan, lids open. Preheat half the oil in a large frying pan. Sauté the onions, garlic and parsley for about 5 minutes (if you are using meat, do this now as well). Add salt, pepper and rice. Mix thoroughly and sauté another 5 minutes. Remove from heat. Blend tomato seeds and pulp previously set aside in the blender and season. Place in small saucepan with remaining oil and bring to a boil for 15 minutes. Stuff tomatoes with spoonfuls of rice mixture to fill halfway. This allows for the expansion of the cooked rice. Pour 2 tbsp. of blended and boiled tomato mixture into each tomato. Pour rest into bottom of pan surrounding the stuffed tomatoes. Place the lids over top the tomatoes and bake in preheated oven at 375 degrees for about 45 minutes. Serve as main dish when made with meat, or as side dish. (You may also choose to eliminate the meat and replace it with such items as feta cheese, black olives, grated zucchini, eggplant, carrots, etc. for variations.)

Serves 6
Time 1 1/2 hours

CHRISTMAS COOKIES
KOURABIEDES

Fried Zucchini
(Kolokithi Tyganito)

8	Small Zucchini, sliced lengthwise
1 cup	Olive Oil
1 cup	Flour
1 tsp.	Salt
1/4 tsp.	Pepper
2	Eggs, lightly beaten
1	Lemon

Method:

Place the flour onto a dinner plate, spreading out evenly. In a large bowl, mix the eggs with a whisk while you pour the juice from 1 lemon into it very slowly. Watch that the mixture does not break up or curdle. Coat zucchini slices in egg mixture, then roll into flour on plate. Preheat a skillet with oil, and when hot, fry the zucchini on both sides until golden brown.

Serves 6
Time 35 minutes

Zucchini a La Greque
(Kolokithi Elliniko)

10	Small Zucchini, cut into thin strips
1 tbsp.	Tarragon, chopped fresh
1 tbsp	Lemon Juice
1	Large Garlic Clove,
1 tbsp.	Parsley, finely chopped
1	Large Tomato, peeled and seeded
1 pinch	Dried Thyme
1 tsp.	Salt
1/4 tsp.	Pepper
1	Bay Leaf
4 tbsp.	Olive Oil
1 cup	Water

Method:

Bring all ingredients to a boil in a heavy saucepan. Reduce heat and simmer gently until zucchini is slightly tender. Remove the bay leaf. Let cool to room temperature, then chill. Serve as appetizer or side dish to any meal.

Serves 4
Time 10 minutes

Stuffed Zucchini
(Kolokithia Gemista)

16	Zucchini, medium-sized
1/2 cup	Olive Oil
1 lb.	Ground Beef, or Lamb (lean)
1 cup	Long Grain Rice
4	Garlic Cloves
1	Large Onion, finely chopped
2	Stalks Celery, finely chopped
1 tbsp.	Fresh Parsley, finely chopped
1 tsp.	Salt
1/2 tsp.	Pepper
1/2 cup	Parmesan Cheese, grated
1 cup	Water

Method:

Rinse the zucchini thoroughly and trim the ends. Slice lengthwise, not too deep, to make a lid. Set aside. Hollow out the centers of each zucchini so they look like little canoes. Place in large baking pan, side by side to cover the bottom. In a large frying pan, preheat the oil over low heat. Sauté the onions, celery, parsley, salt, pepper, ground meat and rice for about 20 minutes, or until brown. Remove from heat and stuff zucchini until 3/4 of the way full. This leaves room for the rice to expand. Preheat oven to 375 degrees. Replace the strips of zucchini to make lids. Brush with oil. Pour a cup of water into the pan, sprinkle with cheese and bake for 45 minutes. Remove when golden brown and serve hot.

Serves 6
Time 1 1/2 hours

CHEESE RINGS
(KOULOURIA ME TYRI)

1/2 cup	Butter
1 cup	Parmesan Cheese, grated
3 tbsp.	Milk
1	Egg
1 1/2 cups	Flour
1 tsp.	Sesame Seeds

Method:

Preheat oven to 350 degrees. Combine the parmesan cheese and flour. Melt butter. Stir in the milk and mix well. Add to the dry ingredients and mix well until soft dough is formed. Cut dough into 24 equal pieces. Roll each piece out to 5" long and pinch together in a circle. Place on ungreased cookie sheet and brush tops with beaten egg, sprinkling them with the sesame seeds. Bake for 25 minutes or until lightly browned. Remove and place on rack to cool.

Serves 15-20
Time 1 1/2 hours

Fisherman's Dinner
(Psarathiko Yevma)

1 lb.	Squid, cleaned and diced
1 lb.	Red Snapper Fillets, cleaned and diced
12	Large Oysters, fresh if possible and cut in half
12	Large Clams, cut in half
8	Large Prawns, cut in half
8	Crab Legs, meat only
12	Black Greek Olives, sliced
1	Large Green Pepper, chopped
1	Large Onion, chopped
4	Celery Stalks, chopped
4	Large Garlic Cloves, minced
1 tsp.	Oregano
1 tsp.	Salt
1 tsp.	Pepper
3 tbsp.	Tomato Paste
2	Medium Fresh Tomatoes, sliced
1 cup	Olive Oil
3 cups	Long Grain Rice
6 cups	Water

Method:

De-bone the squid and clean well, along with the red snapper, prawns, clams, oysters and crab meat. Dice the squid and prawns and half the shellfish. Feather the crab meat into pieces. Preheat the oil in a deep frying pan over medium heat. Sauté the chopped onions, garlic, celery, green peppers and olives for about 10 minutes. Add the oregano, salt and pepper, stirring every few minutes. When golden brown, add all seafood and stir for another 5 minutes. Slice the fresh tomatoes and place on top of the mixture for a few minutes. Remove mixture from heat and set aside. In a large 8 quart casserole dish, add the 6 cups of water and tomato paste and dissolve well. Add the seafood and bring to a boil. Add the uncooked rice and cook until rice is done (about 20 minutes). Do not mix.

Serves 8
Time 1 hour

Salted Dried Fish with Potatoes
(Vakalaos Me Skorthalia)

2 lbs.	Dried White Fish
1/4 cup	Virgin Olive Oil
1/4 cup	Red Wine Vinegar
1	Whole Garlic Clove
6	Medium Potatoes, boiled and mashed
1 tsp.	Salt
1/2 cup	Water

Method:

Cut the fish into squares and place into a bowl with cold water to cover completely. Let stand overnight. Drain, wash and rinse well. Roll in flour. Preheat the oil in a heavy skillet and fry the fish until golden brown on all sides. Place the remaining ingredients, as they are listed, into a mixing bowl and mix at high speed. Stop the mixture every so often to pull the ingredients from sides of bowl. When the mixture is thick and creamy, taste for sharpness. Add a little oil and beat in thoroughly. The garlic and vinegar flavors should dominate. If not, add a little of what is needed. Set aside in the refrigerator for 2 hours until ready to serve. Serve with the fried fish.

Serves 6
Time   1 hour

Mussels with Tomato
(Midia Yiahni)

2 qrts.	Mussels, cleaned and scrubbed
1 cup	Water
1/4 cup	Olive Oil
1/2 cup	Raw Rice
2	Large Onions, chopped
1 cup	Tomato Sauce
1 tsp.	Salt
1/4 tsp.	Pepper

Method:

In a heavy skillet, preheat the oil and brown the onions. Add the tomato sauce, salt and pepper and rice and cook for 5 minutes. Add the water and cook for 10 minutes more. Add the mussels in their shells and cook for 15 minutes, or until rice is tender and mussel shells are open. Add more liquid if necessary.

Serves 4
Time 1 hour

STUFFED ZUCCHINI
KOLOKITHI, GEMISTO

Octopus with Rice
(Oktapothi Pilafi)

2 lbs.	Fresh Octopus, skinned
2	Large Onions, chopped
1/3 lb.	Butter
1	Garlic Clove, minced
1	Bay Leaf
1 tsp.	Oregano
1 tbsp.	Tomato Paste
1-16 oz.	Can Whole Tomatoes
1 cup	White Wine
2 cups	Raw Rice
3 1/2 cups	Water
1 tsp.	Salt
1/4 tsp.	Pepper

Method:

Sauté the onions in 1/4 cup of the butter until golden brown. Add the cubed octopus, oregano, bay leaf and garlic. Cover and simmer for at least 1 hour. Half way through cooking, place the water into a separate saucepan along with 1/2 cup of the broth that the meat is cooking in and 2 tbsp. butter. Bring to a boil, add the rice and cook.. Form the cooked rice into a mold, drop onto a platter and serve with the octopus and sauce over the top. Serve hot.

Serves 4
Time 1 1/2 hours

Oyster Stew
(Strithia Yiahni)

2 qrts.	Oyster, cleaned
1 cup	Water
1 tsp.	Parsley
1/2 cup	Rice
1 cup	Tomato Sauce
2	Large Onions, chopped
1/4 cup	Olive Oil
1 tsp.	Salt
1/2 tsp.	Pepper

Method:

Sauté the onions in olive oil. When brown, add the rice and the tomato sauce, stirring constantly. Cook for about 5 minutes. Add the water and cook for another 10 minutes. Add the oysters, parsley, salt and pepper to taste. Cook for 15 minutes. Test the rice; if tender, the oysters are also cooked. Add more water if needed.

Serves 4
Time 45 minutes

Red Snapper with Sauce
(Barbouni Avgolemono)

4 lbs.	Red Snapper, whole, cleaned and scaled
2	Eggs
2	Lemons, juice only
1/2 cup	Olive Oil
2	Medium Onions, chopped
3 cups	Water
1	Celery Stalk
1 tbsp.	Flour
1 tsp.	Salt
1/2 tsp.	Pepper
6	Parsley Sprigs

Method:

Wash the celery well and chop into 3" pieces. Boil for 5 minutes in 2 cups salted water and drain. In a skillet, sauté the onions, in 1/2 cup oil. Place the celery on top and the fish on top of the celery. Season with salt and pepper. Add 1 cup of water and simmer covered for 20 minutes. Remove the fish and the vegetables and set aside, keeping them warm. Strain the broth to make 1 cup. Set aside as well. Blend together the eggs, lemon juice and the flour in a blender. Add the broth to it. Pour into a saucepan and heat until slightly thick. Lace the snapper with the sauce and garnish with parsley.

Serves 8
Time 1 hour

Seafood in Wine
(Psari Me Krasi)

1 lb.	Small Squid, cleaned
1 lb.	Lobster, meat only
1 lb.	Prawns, cleaned
3 cups	Onions, chopped
1/2 cup	Olive Oil
1 tsp.	Salt
1/2 tsp.	Pepper
1/2 tsp.	Oregano
4	Garlic Cloves, minced
1 cup	Red Wine

Method:

Remove the ink sac, back quill, eyes and teeth from the squid and wash well. Cut crosswise into 1 1/2" pieces. Clean and devein the prawns and cut in half. Cut the lobster meat into 1" cubes. In a saucepan sauté the onions to soften, but not to brown. Add the seafood, salt, pepper and garlic and sauté for 2 minutes. Stir in the wine and the oregano. Cover and let cook for 20 minutes. Serve over rice.

Serves 8
Time 1 hour

Shrimp Spaghetti Au Four
(Garithes Macaroni Fournou)

2 lbs.	Raw Spaghetti
2 lbs.	Shrimp
1/2 cup	Olive Oil
3/4 cup	Onions, chopped
1/2 cup	White Wine
1 lb.	Ripe Tomatoes, peeled and strained
1/2 tbsp.	Parsley, minced
1	Green Pepper, chopped
1 tsp.	Salt
1/2 tsp.	Pepper
3	Tomatoes, fresh and sliced thin for garnish

Method:

Cook spaghetti according to package directions. Leave in a large bowl once drained and set aside. Shell, wash and de-vein the shrimp. In a saucepan preheat the oil and sauté the onions. Add the wine, strained tomatoes, parsley, green pepper, salt and pepper. Cook until sauce thickens. Add the shrimp and cook for 3 minutes. Remove the sauce from the heat and pour over the cooked spaghetti, mixing well. Place into a 12"x9" casserole pan and top with the tomato slices evenly. Bake in a preheated 300 degree oven for 15 minutes. Serve hot.

Serves 10
Time 1 hour

SHRIMP WITH CHEESE
(GARITHES ME TYRI)

1 lb.	Shrimp, peeled and de-veined
1 1/2 cups	Feta Cheese
2 cups	Rice, cooked in advance
1/2 cup	Onions, chopped
1 lb.	Ripe Tomatoes, chopped fine
4 tbsp.	Butter
1 tsp.	Salt
1/2 tsp.	Pepper
1/2 tsp.	Parsley

Method:

Sauté the onions in the butter. Add the salt and pepper. Mix with the cooked rice and spread in a 1 1/2 quart casserole dish. Arrange the shrimp and the cheese on top of the rice. Sprinkle with parsley. Add the tomatoes without any liquid and bake for 35 minutes in a preheated 350 degree oven.

Serves 4
Time 1 hour

Mediterranean Shrimp Casserole
(Garithes Crema)

3 doz.	Shrimp
1	Large Onion, minced
1/3 lb.	Butter
3 tbsp..	Brandy
1 cup	White Wine
2	Large Tomatoes, sliced
1 cup	Chicken Stock
1 tbsp.	Fresh Parsley, chopped
1/4 tsp.	Dill
1	Bay Leaf
1/3 cup	Flour
1/2 cup	Milk
1/2 cup	Feta Cheese, crumbled

Method:

Shell shrimp and poach the shells in water to produce the stock. Set aside. In a large pot, sauté the onions in butter over medium heat. Add the shrimp and cook just until they are pink in color. Flame the brandy and pour it over the shrimp. Add the white wine, tomatoes, chicken stock and herbs. Simmer for 5 minutes. Make the sauce by melting the butter (do not let it brown). Stir in the flour and cook over low heat for 1 minute. Gradually add the milk and the broth from the shrimp and stir to make a creamy, thick sauce. Butter the inside of a quart casserole dish and layer the shrimp and the sauce, sprinkling each layer with feta cheese. Bake for 30 minutes at 450 degrees.

Serves 8
Time 1 hour

Greek-Style Shrimp and Okra
(Bamies Me Garithes)

1 1/2 cups	Green Onions, chopped
6	Garlic Cloves, minced
2/3 cup	Olive Oil
4 cups	Fresh Okra, cut crosswise
2 lbs.	Large Shrimp, cleaned
2 cups	Water
2 cups	Tomato Juice
4	Bay Leaves
2 cups	Canned Tomatoes
1 tsp.	Salt
1/2 tsp	Pepper
1/2 tsp.	Parsley

Method:

Sauté the garlic, onions and okra in oil for about 10 minutes. Stir constantly. Add the shrimp and cook for 5 more minutes. Add the tomato juice, tomatoes, water, bay leaves, salt and pepper. Cover and simmer for 20 minutes. Remove the bay leaves and serve over cooked rice.

Serves 4
Time 45 minutes

Squid in Red Wine Sauce
(Kalamaria Krasi)

3 lbs	Squid
3 cups	Onions, chopped
1/2 cup	Red Wine
1 tsp.	Garlic, minced
1 tsp.	Salt
1/2 tsp.	Pepper

Method:

Clean squid by removing the ink sac, insides, eggs (if any), eyes, teeth and backbone (transparent). Use only the tube of the body and the tentacles. Blanche the squid, then cut each in pieces. In a saucepan cook the onion in the oil until tender. Do not brown. Add the squid and heat through. Add the salt, pepper and garlic and stir. Add the red wine. Cook for 20 minutes. Serve with rice.

Serves 6
Time 1 hour

Shrimp Kebabs
(Garithes Souvlaki)

4 lbs.	Shrimp, cleaned
1/2 cup	Olive Oil
1/4 cup	Lemon Juice
2 tbsp.	Brandy
1/4 tsp.	Salt
1/4 tsp.	Pepper
1/4 tsp.	Oregano
1/4 tsp.	Thyme
1/4 tsp.	Garlic Powder

Method:

Combine all the ingredients and add the shrimp. Mix well and let soak for 3 hours in own juices. Place the shrimp on skewers. Broil over BBQ preheated for 10 minutes. Turn once. Serve with a lemon wedge or on bed of wild rice.

Serves 8
Time 4 hours (including marinate)

CHEESE TRIANGLES
TYROPITAKIA

Greek Pan Fried Smelts
(Tiganites Marithes)

4 doz.	Smelts, medium-sized, cleaned without heads
1 cup	Olive Oil
1 tsp.	Salt
1/2 tsp.	Pepper
1 cup	Flour
1	Lemon, juice only

Method:

Clean and cut the heads from the smelt. Coat with salt, pepper and flour. Heat the olive oil in a large frying pan. Fry the fish until golden brown and crisp on both sides. Drizzle the lemon juice over them and serve with Greek salad and fresh French bread.

Serves 8
Time 1/2 hour

Stuffed Baby Squid
(Kalamaraki Gemisto)

20	Baby Squid, cleaned
6	Anchovy Fillets
4	Sprigs Parsley
2	Eggs, lightly beaten
1 cup	Bread Crumbs
1 tsp.	Salt
1/4 tsp.	Pepper
3 tbsp.	Olive Oil
8	Lemon Wedges

Method:

Cut the tentacles from the squid, chopping them fine. Place them in a blender with the anchovies, garlic and parsley. Combine the eggs, bread crumbs, salt, pepper and oil. Work this mixture into a paste. Stuff the cleaned squid bodies with the mixture and sew shut. Sprinkle with salt and pepper and baste with oil. Cook under a broiler preheated moderately for 15 minutes, turning occasionally and basting with oil. Serve hot garnished with fresh cooked pea pods, lemon wedges and whole sprigs of parsley.

Serves 6
Time 40 minutes

Squid Pilaf
(Kalamaria Me Rizi)

2 lbs.	Small Squid
2 cups	Long Grain Rice
1	Large Onion, chopped
4	Large Garlic Cloves, minced
2	Celery Stalks, diced
1 cup	Tomato Paste
4 cups	Water
1 tsp.	Salt
1/2 tsp.	Pepper
1 tbsp.	Parsley, chopped fresh
1/2 cup	Olive Oil
1	Large Green Pepper, diced

Method:

To clean the squid well, place in a sink full of water. Remove eyes, teeth, backbone, ink sac and innards. Let soak and rinse well to get rid of all ink traces. Set aside. Preheat oil in a heavy skillet over medium heat. Sauté the onions, garlic, celery, green peppers, salt and pepper for about 10 minutes or until golden brown. Add the squid and sauté for another 10 minutes. Sprinkle with parsley and mix well just before removing from heat. Dilute the tomato paste in the 4 cups of water and place in a dutch oven casserole. Transfer the mixture into this as well. Let come to a boil over medium-high heat. Add the 2 cups of raw long grain rice and stir in well. Cover and let cook until rice is tender, about 20 minutes. Stir occasionally. Serve with grated cheese sprinkled over and garnished with fresh parsley sprigs.

Serves 4
Time 2 1/2 hours

STUFFED SQUID TUBES
(KALAMARI YEMISTO)

1 lb.	Squid Tubes, cut to form tubes
4 oz	Crab Meat, chopped fine
4 oz.	Small Shrimps
8 oz.	Small Clams
1	Medium Onion, diced
1 cup	Celery, diced
2	Large Garlic Cloves, minced
2	Medium Tomatoes
1 cup	Olive Oil
1 tsp.	Salt
1 tsp.	Pepper
1 tsp.	Oregano
1 tsp.	Fresh Parsley, chopped
1	Egg

Method:

In a large bowl, combine the onions, garlic, parsley, salt, pepper and oregano. Add the seafood and mix together. Mix in the egg. Work this together to form a thick paste. Stuff the squid body tubes with the paste and set into a 10" casserole pan. Set aside. Cube the 2 fresh tomatoes. Preheat the oil in. a saucepan and simmer the tomatoes for about 20 minutes. Pour this over the squid, then place the fish into a preheated 375 degree oven for about 40 minutes. Serve hot with rice, boiled potatoes and fresh green vegetables.

Serves 4-6
Time 1 1/2 hours

Greek Lemon Trout
(Psari Lemoni Elliniko)

6	Medium Trout
1/2 cup	Olive Oil
1/2 cup	Flour
3	Eggs
2	Lemons
1 tsp.	Salt
1/2 tsp.	Pepper
1 cup	Water

Method:

Clean trout well and cut off heads. Coat fish well on both sides with flour. Preheat half the oil in a heavy skillet over medium heat and fry fish until golden brown. Set aside. In a medium casserole dish, pour the remaining oil, water, salt, pepper, parsley and simmer for 5 minutes on low heat. Beat the eggs and juice the lemons. Add the juice to the eggs slowly, beating constantly to prevent curdling. Then take 2-3 tbsp. of the casserole juices and repeat the same procedure. Combine all juices together in casserole dish, blending constantly once again. The mixture should thicken up. Remove from heat and transfer to a gravy or sauce boat. Lace the fish with the sauce and serve hot with your favorite rice dish.

Serves 6
Time 1 hour

Tomato Marmalade
(Marmelatha Domata)

4 lbs.	Tomatoes, peeled, seeded and chopped
2	Oranges, thick-skinned
2	Whole Lemons
2	Cinnamon Sticks
1 tsp.	Whole Cloves
5 cups	Sugar

Method:

Place the tomato pulp in a colander to drain. Rinse the oranges and the lemons. Remove their skins with a vegetable peeler and cut into julienne strips. Cut off and discard the pith, chop the fruit and discard the seeds. Tie the cinnamon sticks and cloves into a piece of cheesecloth. In an enamel saucepan, place the spice bag, tomato pulp, fruit and peel. Add the sugar and cook over low heat until the sugar is dissolved. Skim off the froth as it accumulates. Increase the heat and boil the mixture for 30 more minutes, or until a candy thermometer measures 222 degrees Fahrenheit. Remove and discard the spice bag and let cool for 10 minutes. Skim the froth again and stir. Pour the marmalade into sterilized heated jars and seal. Set aside to cool to room temperature before storing.

Makes 5 cups
Time 1 1/2 hours

Tzatziki Sauce
(Giaourti Me Agouri)

1 1/2 cups	Plain Yogurt
1	Medium Cucumber
1 tbsp.	Lemon Juice
1	Large Garlic Clove
1 tsp.	Salt
1/4 tsp.	Pepper
1 tbsp.	Fresh Mint, chopped

Method:

Line a strainer with a double layer of cheesecloth. Place over a bowl. Spoon yogurt into it and let stand drain for 2 hours. Peel the cucumber with vegetable peeler so some of the green layer under the skin remains. Cut in half lengthwise and scoop out any seeds. Grate the remaining flesh very fine. Place in the strainer as well and let drain. Combine drained yogurt, cucumber, lemon juice and crushed garlic in a bowl. Season with salt and pepper. Take half the mint and fold into the mixture. Sprinkle remaining over top. Fantastic served with calamari (squid) and vegetable appetizers.

Serves 6-8
Time 40 minutes

Sweet Greek Syrup
(Siropi Eliniko)

2 cups	Sugar
1 cup	Water
1 tbsp.	Lemon Juice
1	Cinnamon Stick
1/4 cup	Honey

Method:

Place the sugar, water, cinnamon stick and lemon juice in a saucepan and bring to a boil. Lower the heat and simmer for about 30 minutes. Remove from heat and stir in the honey. Blend well. This sauce is used for any cookies or sweets that may require soaking in a syrup.

Makes 2 cups
Time 30 minutes

Orzo in Butter Sauce
(Rizi Pasta Saltza)

1 lb.	Orzo Pasta
2/3 cup	Butter
1 tsp.	Salt
6 tbsp.	Parmesan Cheese, grated

Method:

Cook pasta according to package directions. Drain and set aside to keep warm. Place butter in a small saucepan and melt over medium heat until brown. Place in a pasta bowl, along with the orzo, and mix together well. Sprinkle with cheese and serve hot.

Serves 8
Time 45 minutes

Marinade

1 cup	Chicken Stock
1/2 cup	Dry White Wine
1/2 cup	Olive Oil
2 tbsp.	Lemon Juice
2 tbsp.	Shallots, chopped
1/2 tsp.	Peppercorns
1/2 tsp.	Coriander Seed
1/2 tsp.	Garlic, minced
5	Parsley Sprigs
3	Thyme Sprigs
1	Bay Leaf
1/2	Celery Stalk
1/4 tsp.	Salt
1/4 tsp.	Pepper

Method:

Place all ingredients together in a saucepan and bring to a boil. Simmer for about 5 minutes. This can be used to marinate almost anything. Very herbal-tasting marinate, good on pork, chicken and fish.

Makes 2 cups
Time 15 minutes

Orange Sauce
(Saltsa Portocali)

2	Oranges
2 oz.	Grand Marnier (optional)
1 tbsp.	Corn Starch
1 cup	Unsalted Butter
1 cup	White Sugar

Method:

Squeeze juice from 2 oranges. Grate the remaining rind into a small cup and set aside. Place butter in a small saucepan and simmer for a few minutes until melted. Add the orange juice and rind and simmer again. Add the sugar and stir well to dissolve. Let simmer for 15 minutes. Combine the cornstarch with a couple tbsp. of water to dissolve and add to the orange sauce. Stir until it starts to thicken, then remove from heat. Pour into a gravy boat. This is excellent sauce for stuffed turkey, chicken or any other festive fowl you may be serving. Good served over meat and rice.

Serves 6
Time 1/2 hour

Stuffed Grape Leaves
(Dolmathes)

3/4 cup	Olive Oil
3	Large Onions, chopped fine
6	Scallions, diced
1 tsp.	Salt
1/4 tsp.	Pepper
2 tbsp.	Pine Nuts (optional)
1 cup	Long Grain Rice
1 lb.	Ground Beef (optional)
1 tbsp.	Dill
1/2 cup	Fresh Parsley, chopped
3/4 tsp.	Mint, crushed
5 tbsp.	Lemon Juice
12 oz.	Grape Leave, jarred
6	Lemon Wedges
1 cup	Water
	Parsley Sprigs

Method:

Heat half the oil in a heavy saucepan. Sauté the onions and scallions over low heat until soft. Add salt, pepper, pine nuts and raw rice and cook for 10 minutes, stirring occasionally. Add ground beef (if desired), dill, chopped parsley, mint, 2 tbsp. of lemon juice and water. Cover pan and simmer until all liquids are absorbed (about 10 minutes). The rice will be undercooked. Taste for seasoning and adjust accordingly. Set aside. Drain brine from grape leaves and thoroughly rinse them in cool water. Blanch them by dipping in boiling water for about 1 minute. Drain. Separate leaves carefully and cut off thick stems. Place rice mixture in center of leaf and roll like a cabbage roll. Do not roll too tight and make them small. Continue until done. Place fresh parsley sprigs at bottom of large casserole pan. Layer rolls over top. Mix together remaining oil, lemon juice and 2 cups water together and pour over the rolls. Weigh down the rolls with a heat-resistant plate so they do not move while cooking. Water should barely cover the plate. Bring to boil and simmer for 1 1/2 hours. Remove from heat and cool overnight. Serve as appetizer with lemon juice over them, or as main dish, heated or cold.

Serves 6-12
Time 3 hours

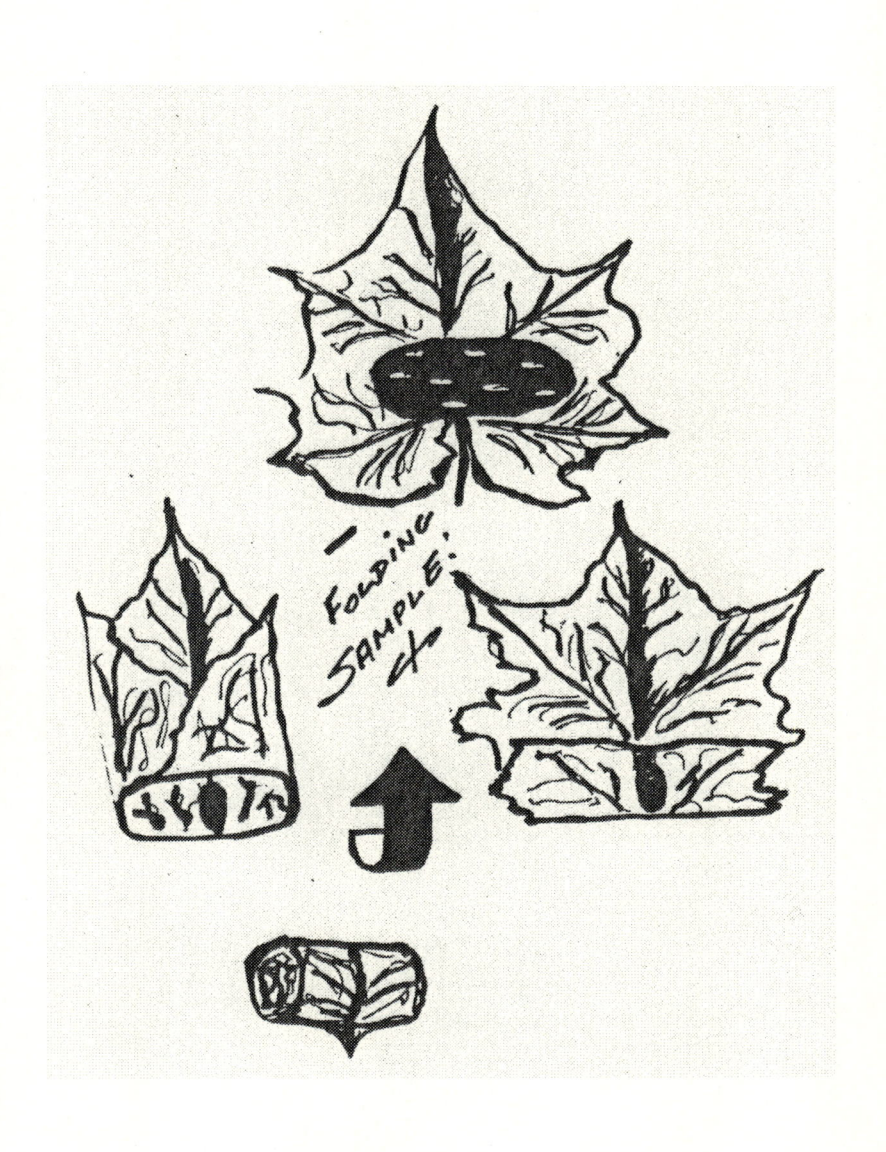

FOLDING NAPKINS

Glossary

ANDITHIA	Endives
ANITHO	Dill
ASPARANGI	Asparagus
ASTAKOS	Lobster
ATZEM PILAF	Meat dish with rice
BAKALIAROS	Salted codfish
BAKLAVA	Phyllo dessert with nuts, spices and syrup
BARBOUNI	Red mallet
BIZELIA	Green peas
DIOSMO	Mint
DOLMATHES	Stuffed grape leaves
FENIKIA	Honey cookies
FILO	Phyllo pastry
FRAPA	Grapefruit
HAVIARI	Caviar
HIRINO	Pork
HORTA	Dandelion greens
KAPAMA	Meat or poultry with onions, tomatoes and cinnamon
KARAMELA	Caramel
KARITHOPITA	Walnut cake
KARPOUZI	Watermelon
KASSERI	Cheese, similar to Swiss, made with goats milk
KEFALOTIRI	Greek cheese, similar to parmesan
KEFTES	Meatballs
KEKI	Cake
KIMINO	Cumin

KOKORIETSI	A mixture of end cuts of lamb and internals grilled and served at Easter time
KOUKIA	Broad beans
KOUNOUPITHI	Cauliflower
KREMA	Custard or pudding
KREMITHIA	Onions
KYTHONI	Quince
LOUKOUMI	Turkish delight
MAIDANO	Parsley
MARITHES	Smelts
MAROULI	Lettuce
MIDIA	Mussels
MILO	Apple
PALAMITHA	Silver fish from Africa
PRASA	Leeks
PELTE	Pudding
PAPIA	Duck
PANTESPANI	Sponge cake
POLITA	Turkish-style (A la polita)
RAVANI	Butter cake with syrup poured over it
REVITHIA	Chick peas
RIGANI	Oregano
ROMI	Rum
SARTHELA	Sardines
SELINO	Celery
SFOGATO	Soufflé
SIKOTI	Liver
SKOUMBRI	Mackerel
SPANAKI	Spinach
TARAMA	Carp roe
TIROPITA	Cheese phyllo pie
TOURSI	Pickled

Appetizers:

Cheese Rings	180
Cheese Triangles	66
Chicken Liver Pate	122
Feta Dip	125
Fish Roe Salad	133
Fried Cheese	123
Fried Mushrooms	124
Fried Zucchini	176
Potatoes and Garlic	170
Salmon Roe Dip	128
Snail Stew	129
Spinach Cheese Puffs	131
Squid Rings	126
Stuffed Grape Leaves	215

Salads:

Bean Salad	134
Chick Pea Salad	135
Country Salad	139
Greek Salad	140
Lentil and Anchovie Salad	141
Vegetable Salad	143
Zucchini Salad	144

Soups:

Bean Soup	145
Cucumber Soup	150
Garden Lentil Soup	155
Greek Tahini Soup	157
Lamb Soup with Egg and Lemon	151

Vegetables:

Baked Artichoke Halves	160
Baked Potatoes in Tomato Sauce	162
Black-Eyed Beans Casserole	163
Fava Beans in Tomato Sauce	165
Greek-Style Braised Artichokes	158
Lentils and Greens	161
Lentils Puree	153
Potatoes Oregano	167
Stuffed Tomatoes	173
Tomatoes and Zucchini	171
Zucchini a La Greque	177

Sauces:

Eggplant Sauce	164
Marinade	213
Orange Sauce	214
Tzatziki Sauce	210

Pasta:

Orzo in Butter Sauce	212

Breads:

Christmas Bread	114
Easter Plait	107
Greek Coffee Biscuits	118
Greek Corn Bread	111
Olive Muffins	81
Pita Bread	20

Pudding:

Greek-Style Grape Pudding	103

Desserts:

Almond Apricot Phyllo Tart	18
Baklava	120
Black Cherry Preserve	116
Butter Cookies	117
Chestnut Fritters	113
Custard Pie	109
Fritter Puffs	104
Greek Apple Pie	16
Greek Halva	98

Greek New Year's Cake	82
Greek Short Bread Cookies	74
Greek Walnut Cake	70
Honey Cheese Pie	99
Honey Cookies	101
Honey Puffs	100
Kadaife	83
Pecan Bars	80
Saragli	76
Sesame Cookies	78
Sweet Greek Syrup	211
Tomato Marmalade	209
Turkish Delight	72
Watermelon Preserve	69
Yogurt Fruit	68

Fish:

Chick Peas with Salmon	137
Fisherman's Dinner	181
Fried Oysters	130
Greek Lemon Trout	207
Greek Pan Fried Smelts	201
Greek-Style Fish Balls	86
Greek-Style Shrimp and Okra	197
Mediterranean Shriimp Casserole	195
Mussels with Tomato	184
Octopus with Rice	186
Oyster Stew	188
Red Snapper with Sauce	189
Salted Dried Fish with Potatoes	183

Seafood in Wine	191
Shrimp Kebabs	199
Shrimp Spaghetti Au Four	192
Shrimp with Cheese	194
Squid in Red Wine Sauce	198
Squid Pilaf	203
Stuffed Baby Squid	202
Stuffed Squid Tubes	205

Poultry:

Baked Chicken Breasts	43
Chicken Phyllo Pie	7
Chicken Pie	46
Chicken Rolls	44
Festive Greek Turkey	57
Greek Garden Chicken	52
Greek-Style Chicken and Soup	147
Greek-Style Chicken with Orzo	48
Mediterranean Chicken and Okra	50
Roast Goose	55
Stuffed Chicken with Lamb	54

Meats:

Baked Lamb Islander	60
Baked Lamb with Cabbage	61
Beef and Peas	36
Beef Stew	33
Beef Stuffed Pita	34

EGGPLANT AND LAMB MEATBALLS	32
FILET OF LAMB	64
GREEK LAMB AND ONIONS	10
GREEK PORK WITH CELERY	92
GREEK SAUSAGES	97
GREEK-STYLE BBQ LAMB CHOPS	9
GREEK-STYLE LAMB CHOPS	87
HAM WITH PASTA	88
LAMB FRICASSEE	25
LAMB PHYLLO PIE	21
LAMB STEW WITH BROAD BEANS	23
LAMB STUFFED CABBAGE	30
LAMB WITH ARTICHOKES	63
LAMB WITH BAKED ORZO	12
LAMB WITH CAULIFLOWER	119
LAMB WITH LENTILS	28
LAMB WITH WINE SAUCE	26
LEG OF LAMB ELAINE	14
LIVER IN WINE SAUCE	38
PORK CUTLETS IN SAUCE	90
POTATO MUSAKA	168
RABBIT WITH GARLIC	59
ROAST PORK	94
STEWED VEAL STEAKS	41
STUFFED PORK LOIN	95
STUFFED ZUCCHINI	178
VEAL AND PASTA	39
VEAL WITH OLIVES	40

Index

Almond Apricot Phyllo Tart	18
Baked Artichoke Halves	160
Baked Chicken Breasts	43
Baked Lamb Islander	60
Baked Lamb with Cabbage	61
Baked Potatoes in Tomato Sauce	162
Baklava	120
Bean Salad	134
Bean Soup	145
Beef and Peas	36
Beef Stew	33
Beef Stuffed Pita	34
Black Cherry Preserve	116
Black-eyed Beans Casserole	163
Butter Cookies	117
Cheese Rings	180
Cheese Triangles	66
Chestnut Fritters	113
Chick Pea Salad	135
Chick Peas with Salmon	137
Chicken Liver Pate	122
Chicken Phyllo Pie	7

Chicken Pie	46
Chicken Rolls	44
Christmas Bread	114
Country Salad	139
Cucumber Soup	150
Custard Pie	109
Easter Plait	107
Eggplant and Lamb Meatballs	32
Eggplant Sauce	164
Fava Beans in Tomato Sauce	165
Festive Greek Turkey	57
Feta Dip	125
Filet of Lamb	64
Fish Roe Salad	133
Fisherman's Dinner	181
Fried Cheese	123
Fried Mushrooms	124
Fried Oysters	130
Fried Zucchini	176
Fritter Puffs	104
Garden Lentil Soup	155
Greek Apple Pie	16
Greek Coffee Biscuits	118
Greek Corn Bread	111
Greek Garden Chicken	52
Greek Halvah	98
Greek Lamb and Onions	10
Greek Lemon Trout	207
Greek New Year's Cake	82
Greek Pan Fried Smelts	201
Greek Pork with Celery	92
Greek Salad	140

GREEK SAUSAGES	97
GREEK SHORT BREAD COOKIES	74
GREEK TAHINI SOUP	157
GREEK WALNUT CAKE	70
GREEK-STYLE BBQ LAMB CHOPS	9
GREEK-STYLE BRAISED ARTICHOKES	158
GREEK-STYLE CHICKEN AND SOUP	147
GREEK-STYLE CHICKEN WITH ORZO	48
GREEK-STYLE FISH BALLS	86
GREEK-STYLE GRAPE PUDDING	103
GREEK-STYLE LAMB CHOPS	87
GREEK-STYLE SHRIMP AND OKRA	197
HAM WITH PASTA	88
HONEY CHEESE PIE	99
HONEY COOKIES	101
HONEY PUFFS	100
KADAIFE	83
LAMB FRICASSEE	25
LAMB PHYLLO PIE	21
LAMB SOUP WITH EGG AND LEMON	151
LAMB STEW WITH BROAD BEANS	23
LAMB STUFFED CABBAGE	30
LAMB WITH ARTICHOKES	63
LAMB WITH BAKED ORZO	12
LAMB WITH CAULIFLOWER	119
LAMB WITH LENTILS	28
LAMB WITH WINE SAUCE	26
LEG OF LAMB ELAINE	14
LENTIL AND ANCHOVIE SALAD	141
LENTILS AND GREENS	161
LENTILS PUREE	153
LIVER IN WINE SAUCE	38

Marinade	213
Mediterranean Chicken and Okra	50
Mediterranean Shrimp Casserole	195
Mussels with Tomato	184
Octopus with Rice	186
Olive Muffins	81
Orange Sauce	214
Orzo in Butter Sauce	212
Oyster Stew	188
Pecan Bars	80
Pita Bread	20
Pork Cutlets in Sauce	90
Potato Musaka	168
Potatoes and Garlic	170
Potatoes Oregano	167
Rabbit with Garlic	59
Red Snapper with Sauce	189
Roast Goose	55
Roast Pork	94
Salmon Roe Dip	128
Salted Dried Fish with Potatoes	183
Saragli	76
Seafood in Wine	191
Sesame Cookies	78
Shrimp Kebabs	199
Shrimp Spaghetti Au Four	192
Shrimp with Cheese	194
Snail Stew	129
Spinach Cheese Puffs	131
Squid in Red Wine Sauce	198
Squid Pilaf	203
Squid Rings	126

Stewed Veal Steaks	41
Stuffed Baby Squid	202
Stuffed Chicken with Lamb	54
Stuffed Grape Leaves	215
Stuffed Pork Loin	95
Stuffed Squid Tubes	205
Stuffed Tomatoes	173
Stuffed Zucchini	178
Sweet Greek Syrup	211
Tomato Marmalade	209
Tomatoes and Zucchini	171
Turkish Delight	72
Tzatziki Sauce	210
Veal and Pasta	39
Veal with Olives	40
Vegetable Salad	143
Watermelon Preserve	69
Yogurt Fruit	68
Zucchini a La Greque	177
Zucchini Salad	144

Printed in the United States
50757LVS00002B/4-51